ETHICA DIALECTICA

ETHICA DIALECTICA
A STUDY OF ETHICAL OPPOSITIONS

by

HOWARD P. KAINZ

1979

MARTINUS NIJHOFF

THE HAGUE/BOSTON/LONDON

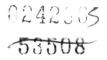

ISBN 90 247 2078 8

PRINTED IN THE NETHERLANDS

TABLE OF CONTENTS

INTRODUCTION

"Dialectic" is a fulcrum word. Aristotle attacked this belief, saying that the dialectic was only suitable for some purposes – to enquire into men's beliefs, to arrive at truths about eternal forms of things, known as *Ideas*, which were fixed and unchanging and constituted reality for Plato. Aristotle said there is also the method of science, or "physical" method, which observes physical facts and arrives at truths about substances, which undergo change. This duality of form and substance and the scientific method of arriving at facts about substances were central to Aristotle's philosophy. Thus the dethronement of dialectic from what Socrates and Plato held it to be was absolutely essential for Aristotle, and "dialectic" was and still is a fulcrum word ...

I think it was Coleridge who said everyone is either a Platonist or an Aristotelian ... Plato is the essential Buddha-seeker who appears again and again in each generation, moving onward and upward toward the "one." Aristotle is the eternal motorcycle mechanic who prefers the "many."

R. Pirsig, *Zen and the Art of Motorcycle Maintenance*

Today our long-standing and time hallowed confidence in the "scientific method," and its ability to yield irrefutable, objective, self-consistent factual "truths" seems as robust and healthy as ever; but there has also appeared on the horizon just a hint here and there of unsettling challenges, and just a few foreboding intimations that all may not be completely right and well with the method that has come to be synonmous with the progress and sophistication of the Western world. Three "hints" or "intimations" come to mind: Gödel's theorem on mathematics, which shattered a century-long quest for a proof of the complete self-consistency of mathematical axioms, by producing a formula showing the exact opposite; Heisenberg's Indeterminacy Principle in physics, which shows the impossibility of obtaining completely "objective" results, especially in microcosmic physical research; and a certain dissatisfaction with discrete and isolated factual analyses, which has led innovative researchers on psychology, political science, sociology, international relations, and other disciplines to resort to various forms of "systems analysis" to try, as it were, to offset and counterbalance the excessive concentration on minutiae that seems to be a kind of "side' effect" of the doubtlessly beneficial employment of the scientific method itself.

Ernst Cassirer in his *Determinism and Indeterminism in Modern Physics* (1956) has tried to draw out some of the implications of Heisenberg's principle specifically with regard to philosophy, but for the most part one has to admit that no major countercurrents on par with the three above-mentioned developments have emerged to undermine or unsettle the confidence which *philosophers* have in their own version of the "scientific method." This version, to its credit, transcends mere parochial Baconian concentration on experimentation and systematic observation and emphasizes more broadly 1) an adherence to "facts" of some sort, if only facts about linguistic usage; and 2) a belief in the reliability of inductive and deductive logic (these two types of logic being used in varying proportions, depending on one's philosophical persuasions) to produce definite conclusions verifiable by the scientifico-philosophical community at large.

This general interpretation of "what it means to do philosophy scientifically" has its "roots," as Pirsig points out at length in his book, in the influence of Aristotle, who, although he was not above some youthful experimentation with dialogic-dialectical methodology nor adverse to allowing the "non-scientific" "dialectical" consideration of pros and cons to play a subordinate, "propadeutic" role in the eventual development of truly "scientific" demonstrations, nevertheless become patently impatient with the seemingly indirect and circuitous nature of dialectic, and came to employ almost exclusively his "scientific" method. At the outset of his *Nichomachean Ethics*, he admits that ethics is a particularly difficult arena for producing scientifically accurate conclusions, but he insists nevertheless that, if we are willing to settle for something less than mathematical exactitude, we can still attain a satisfactory degree of "scientific" accuracy in human sciences like ethics.

For Plato, on the other hand, who in his turn had been strongly influenced by Socrates, dialectic was the "methodology of choice," the truly "scientific" approach to truth, and the only approach that recognized the human situation, i.e. those endemic oppositions between the sensible and the intelligible, the many and the one, becoming and being, which unliberated human beings were caught up in.

By and large, it is in the footsteps of Aristotle that later Western philosophers have followed, rather than Plato. To be sure, some philosophers such as Cicero, Machiavelli, Spinoza, Malebranche, Berkeley, Hume, Fichte, and Schelling have written some philosophical dialogues, but for the most part major philosophical figures in the West have not employed dialectic of any sort *systematically* in developing their own philosophical insights.

This generalization having been made, two significant exceptions come to mind: Aquinas (1225–1274) and Hegel (1770–1831). The medieval philosopher-theologian Thomas Aquinas is not usually thought of under the rubric of "dialectician," but one may say that he stands out as one who took Aristotle's casual admonitions about the "propadeutic" value of dialectical thinking much more seriously than did Aristotle himself. In Aquinas' major work, the *Summa theologiae*, for example, no premises are broached, and no conclusions are reached in any of the articles without a thorough and systematic recapitulation and sifting of the various opposing theories then prevailing on a single issue.

But it is G.W.F. Hegel who, having successfully systematized some pathfinding efforts on the part of two predecessors (Kant and Fichte) and a contemporary (Schelling) is rightly considered to be the foremost exemplar of systematically dialectical philosophy after Plato. There is some disagreement among interpreters as to whether the predominant thing in Hegel is a concentration on oppositions as objective "subject-matter" or a subjective methodology intent on discovering and even generating opposition; but there is concerted agreement that the outstanding feature of Hegel's philosophy is the systematization and almost ritualization of oppositions and contradictions, for the purpose of arriving at a state of truth which emerges from, but also transcends, all the opposites. Marx, Kierkegaard, and Sartre, all of whom were heavily influenced by Hegel, evince in their own writings this or that aspect of the Hegelian dialectic, but are not themselves self-consciously, systematically, and consistently dialectical in the way, and to the degree, that Hegel was.

If we would be pressed to pinpoint the essential characteristics of "dialectic" as manifested in the few very different philosophies cited above as examples, we might say that at the minimum a dialectical philosophy involves the epistemological recognition that contradictions and oppositions are not merely negative and messy obstacles, but can provide the necessary and sufficient impetus or catalyst to the discovery and proper presentation of truth; and, at the maximum it involves 1) (here Plato and Hegel especially come to mind) the explicit assertion that "reality" is ontologically grounded in, or constituted from, certain oppositions, and 2) (here only Hegel comes to mind) a methodological commitment to expressing conclusions in terms of, and in the explicit context of, the oppositions out of which they have been generated.

Ethica Dialectica as a whole is "dialectical" only in the "minimal" sense adumbrated above, although one of the characters in the dialogue (Cranston) would also tend towards dialectic in the twofold "maximal" connotations mentioned. But Cranston's tendency is moderated, if not frustrated, by the presence of the other character, Turner. Both characters, however, adhere to a basic presupposition that dialectics in the "minimal" sense may be an important supplement to the various "scientific" approaches prevailing in contempory ethics.

The literary vehicle employed exclusively in the body of this book is dialogue, the peculiarly Platonic instrument for dialectic. In the course of these dialogues, it is Turner who represents an empirico-analytic approach in contemporary ethics (in William James' terminology, the "tough-minded" type of philosopher), but as it turns out finds some difficulty in reconciling his bias for an empirically and naturalistically grounded ethics (normative utilitarianism) with his equally strong bias towards logical and linguistic precision. Cranston, on the other hand, represents the idealistic or "tender-minded" ethicist, who, though not completely convinced by the Kantian appeal to "pure duty," still believes there is something of an a priori or intuitive element in the determination of moral values, and strives in various ways to overcome the handicap which he, in common perhaps with some contemporary phenomenologists and existentialists (most of whom, however, would not recognize themselves as being "handicapped" in any way), is laboring under – namely, the onus of having to justify his very subjective insights in "scientific" ways intelligible and acceptable to an empirically-oriented cultural and philosophical milieu.

At the end of these dialogues, Cranston and Turner in an Epilogue will review the course of their arguments to determine what, if any, modifications of their respective positions are demanded as a result of the concessions, qualifications and clarifications they have made during the course of the discussions.

A knowledge of historical philosophers and some basic ethical terminology current nowadays is for the most part presupposed in the dialogues that follow. However, to supply necessary background information for the beginning student who may be using this book, historical notes and explanations of technical terms are given by means of footnotes and a Glossary of names and subjects, in an Appendix at the end of the book.

CHAPTER I

GOOD AND EVIL

Then Yahweh God gave the man this admonition, "You may eat indeed of all the trees in the garden of Paradise. Nevertheless of the tree of the knowledge of good and evil you are not to eat, for on the day you eat of it you shall most surely die."

Genesis, II, 16–17

CRANSTON: This passage has always intrigued me. The idea seems to be that God is forbidding man to do evil. But the knowledge of evil can't be separated from the knowledge of good, and vice versa. Thus God in this bible story ends up forbidding man to know *good* as well as evil – which sounds strange to our moralistic ears.

TURNER: Let us not rush into biblical exegesis too quickly. In order to determine the meaning of a passage like this, one would have to have access to a lot of information – not only about the context of the story, but also about the identity of the writer and his intentions, and the way that an expression like "the knowledge of good and evil" was utilized in his language and his culture. "The knowledge of good and evil" could be a shorthand expression or euphemism for sexual intercourse. Some Freudians interpret it this way. Or it might be their idiomatic way of referring to magic or sorcery or wizardry. Some take it as synonymous with full self-consciousness and free rationality, which God, at least as perceived and interpreted by primitive man, wanted to keep jealously for himself (although he could not resist the temptation to increase his own enjoyment of his own prerogatives by dangling them as a "prize" before the eyes of his cowering and incompetent creatures).

You yourself seem to be taking the passage in a moral sense – i.e. "good and evil" being roughly equivalent to "right and wrong," and "knowledge" being equivalent to consciousness in the sense of "conscience" – but it does not necessarily have that signification.

CRANSTON: I see what you mean, but I think there is ample evidence that the passage does, indeed, have moral significance – for the writer and his generation, as well as us. If one reads a little further in *Genesis*, he finds that this is reputed to be one of the first laws imposed on man, and that the breaking of the law is forbidden. A moral sense, at least of a primitive sort, seems to be implied here.

TURNER: That would be true if the "law" in this case was what some call a "natural law,"[1] i.e. something the flouting of which would not be consonant with the nature of man. But I see nothing more than what we call "positive law"[2] here. Some external agent, who happens to be "God" in this case, imposes a law, and the subjects must tow the line "or else." No moral sense need be involved. Pragmatism, the instinct of self-preservation and the fear of punishment would suffice to explain man's adherence to the imposed rules.

CRANSTON: I admit that the command has some of the earmarks of a "positive law." It could even be taken as a kind of dietary restriction: "don't eat this particular type of food." But, on the other hand, eating from "the tree of the knowledge of good and evil" should not lightly be placed in the same category as eating pork or animals classified as "unclean"; and the fact that God at the beginning of this creation story enunciates this solemn command to the "first man" – certainly implies that adherence to the command has some importance for the maintenance of the integrity of human *nature* in its pristine purity.

TURNER: I will accept, for the sake of argument, your contention that the command here is meant in a moral sense. Granted this, it seems not just "strange" but outlandish to me that "the knowledge of good and evil" – what we would call "moral knowledge" – is *forbidden*. How can you make that jibe with *any* respectable idea of God?

CRANSTON: Some exegetes, in explaining this apparent incongruity, differentiate between theoretical and practical knowledge. Theoretical knowledge is not forbidden, they say. Only practical "knowledge" – i.e. actually doing or practising evil.

TURNER: Very well, if you want to take evil in the "practical" sense, you have to take good in the same sense. Why would God forbid man to accomplish or practise moral *good?* That seems a little "out of character" for God, you must admit.

CRANSTON: Not necessarily. There may be other goods more important than moral good. The writer of Genesis might be one of the first, but not the only writer to maintain that moral good and the knowledge of it must be subordinated to some higher good. In this case, it seems obvious to me that the "higher good" in question is a kind of religious or mystical union of man with God and/or nature. What *we* call moral thinking – something that involves calculation of right and wrong, merits and demerits – might be considered relatively evil in comparison to that higher good, although relatively good in comparison to some inferior way of life – e.g. mere pleasure-seeking.

TURNER: I must say I'm surprised to hear you talking about relativities. I've never thought of you as a relativist. I'm not adverse to this line of thought; but if *I* were to try to explain how moral knowledge could be relatively "evil" in this context, I would say that it is subordinated to an aesthetic[3] good – the simple enjoyment of the pleasures of primitive life. The author of *Genesis* (like the authors of "creation stories" in many non-Hebraic cultures) seems to be hankering after the innocent, childish enjoyment of life that peoples were supposed to have had before the advent of the complications of civilization and the responsibilities of human maturity. He is telling us, in effect, "something must have happened way-back-when, to cause our life to be so encumbered with difficult or impossible moral restrictions at present."

CRANSTON: I won't argue this point. The "good" in comparison to which moral good becomes an evil might very well be best classified as an "aesthetic" rather than a "religious" way of existing. The point is, moral good here is thought to pale in the face of some other preeminent good, and becomes "evil" in comparison to the latter.

TURNER: Would you be willing to generalize from that, further? I mean, would you go on to assert that evil, in general, is just some good which has been de facto subordinated to a higher good?

CRANSTON: I don't know if I could substantiate that as a generalization. However, I tend in that direction intuitively or instinctively. I certainly wouldn't want to maintain that evil is some sort of negative entity existing in its own right in a sort of Manichean opposition to good.

TURNER: I have a problem for you. Let us suppose that "evil" simply means a good which is relatively inferior to some other good. All there are, are goods arranged hierarchically in a Plotinian manner,[4] so that those lower down on the hierarchy are called unequivocally "evil" while those definitely on the top are called definitely "good." Agreed? Now, in virtue of what do we maintain this hierarchical arrangement? I mean, what is the criterion we use to determine whether some "good" is to be placed toward the top or the bottom of the hierarchy? It would be some idea of perfection, of the absolutely perfect good. Right? And so it would boil down to this: Only this idea would be *the* good. And it would be used as the measure for evaluating the goodness of everything else. Your position concerning the hierarchy seems to place you in that ideological corner. Do you feel comfortable there?

CRANSTON: I would opt for something less Platonic.[5] The good could be considered a quality actually in things, like sweetness, which some things share in more than others; or pervading things, like light, which some objects reflect more than others. We have ideas concerning the quantity of sweetness in things, or the extent to which various objects reflect light.

TURNER: If only "goodness" were a nicely objective and sufficiently measurable quality like sweetness or light, I think your analogy might be useful. But, as you know, there is some disagreement about that. I doubt if you would agree with Jeremy Bentham[6] that the amount of goodness in things or actions can be determined with some exactitude by calculating the amount of pleasure they bring. If you would accept that theory, all we would need to measure the goodness in things would be to take some objective response – for example the dilation of the eyes where the light remains constant – that is definitely connected with the feeling of pleasure, and use that as an index for your measurement ...

CRANSTON: No. My eyes don't dilate when I contemplate Bentham's theory. It seems too simplistic to me. I should think it is obvious to most people, hedonists aside, that judgements about what is good often lead us to reject something more pleasurable in favor of something less pleasurable.

TURNER: You mean, reject some crass or unsophisticated pleasure in favor of a "sublimated" pleasure?

CRANSTON: Very well. I can see that there are already presuppositions operative in the present discussion – presuppositions that presumably are already supplying the criteria for our respective hierarchies of good and evil. And I trust that during the course of our discussions at least some of these presuppositions will be disclosed. But for the present, I just want to make the general point that, *whatever* criterion we use for determining the relative good in things, goodness admits of many degrees, and "evil" is simply a good of definitely inferior degree.

TURNER: My so-called "personal hierarchy" of values may turn out to be simply a reflection of general values espoused in my social environment. At any rate, even if you do find some kind of hierarchy in my thinking, I don't think you will find that "evil" is simply reducible to those things which are on the lower eschelons of that hierarchy. I should think that a little consultation with our own subjective but commonplace experiences would keep us from saying *that*. I mean, there are some horrible, grotesque evils in the world – little children being slaughtered, innocent people being enslaved, talents being ignored or trampled on. If philosophers start maintaining that such realities are manifestations of "good," albeit to an inferior degree, I'm afraid that our "common man" or "man in the street" will laugh the philosophers out of court, so to speak, and with justice ...

CRANSTON: Try to consider this as dispassionately as possible. History, recent as well as ancient, is strewn with tragedies and catastrophes. But we humans have developed the ability of saying "however." I mean, after these terrible events take place, we say "that was a terrible slaughter, however it had the effect of uniting people to prevent occurrences of such things in the future," or "that was a horrible earthquake, however it finally provided the motivation for scientists from all the world to put their heads together to determine the cause of earthquakes, with a view to prevention in the future." Things like that. In other words, every evil has some good aspect. I think it would be impossible to conceptualize an absolute, unmitigated and unqualified "evil."

TURNER: Here you are clearly making the determination of good and evil a very subjective matter. The attribution of goodness to many tragic events depends on our ability to come up with "howevers." It doesn't seem to matter to you whether there are any objective "howevers," or beneficient factors, in the environment. You presume that they will turn up, if only people look for them. One gets the impression that the key to the dependability and omnipresence of your "howevers," is that they can be manufactured out of very skimpy materials, indeed; or even miraculously out of nothing.

CRANSTON: You wouldn't want me to say that goodness could exist without any reference to human consciousness, human appetite and human evaluations, would you? (– As if goodness were ever some unchanging thing-in-itself,[7] impervious to human needs, desires and expectations!).

TURNER: No, goodness is not a thing-in-itself; but neither is anything else. The thing-in-itself is a pure extreme manufactured by philosophers. But something does not have to be a "thing-in-itself" to be objective.

CRANSTON: I don't think it is warranted to classify me as a "subjectivist"[8] simply because I emphasized the fact that "goodness" implies a reference to human consciousness. A long time ago John Locke pointed out that certain "secondary qualities"[9] – such as color, sound and taste – by definition imply the presence and operation of human consciousness; and they let him off, scot-free. No one accused him of subjectivism. Understand me correctly. I'm not saying that moral goodness is something that emerges full-blown from the infinite resources of the creative human mind. There must, for example, be suitable materials (human actions) and human consciousness must be applied to these materials, before designations of moral good can even become possible. But, that being said, it is also important to insist that people by their specifically moral attractions *constitute* the various types of moral good they speak about. The same principle applies to non-moral goods. I admit that there must be extended materials, light and heat, etc. to make sensory goods possible; that there must be a system of economic and social relations to make some goods potentially "useful"; and so forth. But to actualize these potentialities, the subjective element is a *sine qua non*. For I as an individual must partially constitute objects as sensory goods by my attention to, and perception of, them; and as useful goods, by the uses I ascribe to them; I render certain actions good morally or religiously by my moral or religious intentions; I, together with others in my community and culture, come to a consensus about the utility or value of certain states or ways of living, and we call these our "common goods"; and so forth.

TURNER: I'm not sure whether your analogy with the Lockean theory of perception is very viable. Perception is largely passive, i.e. a kind of receptivity. But the "subject matter" we are concerned with here is essentially an activity – human behavior.

CRANSTON: The main reason why I cited the example of secondary qualities was to show how active we are even in something like perception which appears at first blush to be characterized by passivity and receptivity. But creative human *behavior* does not even take on the deceptive aura of passivity; and in our assessment of it, it should be even easier to discern the essential role of subjectivity. Just as in eating it is our gustatory attraction to this or that type of food that accounts for the fact that we call it "good," so also it is our attraction to the thought of this or that kind of behavior that leads us to pronounce it good, i.e. morally good.

TURNER: I don't know about you, but personally I prefer the experimental method, at least in eating. I may be attracted to a morsel but pronounce it "bad" after just one bite.

CRANSTON: I'm not denying that experiences such as that affect our ideas of attractiveness. They are certainly subject to change, on the basis of cumulative experience. But it is still the *attractiveness* of the ideas we distill from our own experience, the experience of others, intuitions or what-not, that is responsible for our designations of good and bad.

TURNER: Then why don't you talk consistently about the "attractiveness" of the ideas rather than the "attraction" which we have in regard to these ideas. The former expression at least has an objective aspect to it, while the latter sounds excessively subjective.

CRANSTON: Because they are *our* ideas; we formulate them and call them good in accord with the character of our attraction. They don't just plop ready-made in front of our mind's eye. At least mine don't. This may sound excessively subjective to you. But I'm sure you wouldn't want to maintain that certain objects or species of behavior could be good even if no one in the world could find the least attractiveness in them.

TURNER: That assertion can be turned upside down: If there were no intrinsically good objects or species of behavior, no one could feel any "attraction" whatsoever.

CRANSTON: An "intrinsically good" object or species of behavior is a contradiction in terms. It's like talking about something being "intrinsically beautiful." Good, like beauty, is primarily a subjective designation.

TURNER: But surely some types of beauty are more objective, i.e. less esoteric, than others. And the same would apply to good. I think that even you and I might be able to agree that certain types of behavior are "objectively" evil.

CRANSTON: Yes, but not because they are "less esoteric." What would constitute them as "objectively evil" would be their *real* disharmony with my fundamental attractions. Thus, ideas of human behavior that are less attractive to us are either matters of indifference, or tolerated as manifestations of a certain pluralism in moral codes or values. Ideas of human behavior that are radically repulsive to us will be dubbed "evil", even "objectively evil." The character of our repulsions will of course be proportioned to the character of our attractions. A strong attraction will result in an "equal and opposite" repulsion for that which contradicts or fundamentally frustrates the object of our attraction; and so forth.

TURNER: This schema of yours is excessively simplified. We often experience competing and even contradictory attractions. Let's say you experience two contradictory attractions, x and y, and you choose x over y. Are we to conclude that your "real" attraction was for x all along?

CRANSTON: Not necessarily. The proof of the pudding is not always in the eating. My choice of x may be an instance of succumbing to a passing and superficial attraction, whereas I really prefer y. If I regret the action, I am officially categorized as a wrongdoer or sinner, but I retain my former attraction and the moral position I took on the basis of this attraction.

TURNER: Some other person may do x and congratulate himself on doing the supremely moral thing, as contrasted with y, for which he fells a repugnance. How am I to know which of you to follow on the road to morality?

CRANSTON: You have to follow your own road, of course; in other words, you cannot become moral without constant reference to your *own* feelings or attractions. But I recognize that there are problems we have to go into, problems of the same sort. Actually, you've just pointed out the tip of the iceberg. Ideas of what is morally good seem to differ not only from person to person but from place to place and generation to generation. One must also eventually take into account cultural and environmental influences, genetic endowments, and many other variables. But if we try to juggle all these considerations at once, we'll get nowhere. For the time being, I would just like to establish the basic principle that in some way, shape or form, the key to defining moral good is to be found somewhere in the vicinity of an understanding of human attractions.

TURNER: I'm willing to be patient and consider these problems one by one, but you've opened the door just long enough to give me a glimpse of things to come. I'm suspicious of the apparent nonchalance with which you consider the possibility of evil being subjectively alchemized into good, and so forth. If we are going to contribute to ethics as a science, we must stop here and there to get our definitions straight, check for consistency, etc. I don't expect our discussions to result in a dull still-life portrait, but I'm not really for an action-packed movie either.

CRANSTON: I agree in the necessity for clear definitions, consistency, and so forth. But I would ask you also not to be prejudiced at the outset towards dialectical considerations, i.e. treatments which are concerned with opposites *as* opposites, and which strive to understand the laws governing the interrelationship of opposites.

TURNER: It strikes me that God may have had good reasons, after all, for forbidding the knowledge of good and evil in *Genesis*. He probably had in mind ethicists like you who would get so enamoured of the "... and ..." connecting the good and evil that they would risk forgetting about the good and the evil which were connected in the first place. In other words, God may have been taking a stand for analytic clarity.

But seriously, I don't think that one can learn much about the intermingling of, or interrelationship between opposites like good and evil, unless we are careful to identify these and differentiate them from one another at the outset.

CRANSTON: Sometimes this process of identification and differentiation is possible only in a "dialectical" context. I would like to use an example from atomic physics to illustrate what I mean: I am thinking of Heisenberg's Indeterminacy principle,[10] which was developed to account for the fact that in quantum physics particles are continually being transformed into waves and waves into particles. According to this principle, the position and momentum (or velocity) of a particle are absolutely relative to each other. If we focus with our instruments on the position of a particle, all we are doing is artificially increasing the amplitude of a wave so that it looks like a particle with a specific location. If, on the other hand, we focus on the velocity of a particle, all we are doing in this case is artificially spreading out a "particle" into a wave so that its wavelength becomes more regular and hence measurable in terms of velocity. But we cannot know both aspects simultaneously, and we can only know one in terms of the other.

Now there seems to be an analogous situation in regard to our knowledge of good and evil. As our knowledge of human nature and behavior becomes more sophisticated morally, we realize that "good intentions" can be a smoke screen for culpable ignorance of circumstances, that the universally accepted mores of one generation become the unforgivable sin of later generations, that the immoralist of today becomes the moral hero of tomorrow, that the "good consequences" of a popularly acclaimed moral stance become the bitter pill that has to be swallowed when the ulterior reverberations of these consequences begin to appear, and so forth. And so this is where dialectics comes in (analogously to the way the Heisenberg principle operates in microphysics) to emphasize that an important aspect of moral science is to trace these constant metamorphoses of good into evil and vice versa. We can't of course, hope to formulate any precise mathematical laws about these transitions; but we can be optimistic about understanding some of the characteristic ways the transitions take place, the conditions that bring them about, the catalysts that accelerate them, and so forth. But just as the quantum physicist has to have very precise ideas of the difference between particles and waves and position and momentum, before he can begin to understand the dynamics of their mutual transition into one another; so also the ethicist has to have some basic and dependable working definitions of moral good and evil before beginning his investigations. I could point out other parallels with the Indeterminacy principle: The principle indicates that it is impossible to have strictly objective knowledge, since the subjective standpoint and methodology of the observer must be taken explicitly into account and included in the report of one's investigations; and I am saying that a consideration of the mechanism of subjective attractions is a *sine qua non* for elaborating the idea of the good. The Indeterminacy principle also leads into the "bootstrap hypothesis," which holds that no physical entities or reactions should be considered in isolation but can be understood only in their total context; and I have similarly pointed out the necessity for taking the idea of moral good not only in the context of moral evil, but in its relationship with other kinds of good and evil, etc.

TURNER: I find these parallels very interesting, Cranston. But of course we can't make any jump from a principle that has been proven to be of value only in atomic physics to wholesale ethical applications. Philosophy has to apply its own "testing apparatus." And I have just thought of a suitable test for some of the ideas you have just been propounding concerning the nature of moral good.

CHAPTER II

"IS" AND "OUGHT"

> [Morality] consists not in any *matter of fact* which can be dis-
> covered by the understanding ... Can there be any difficulty
> in proving that vice and virtue are not matters of fact, whose
> existence we can infer by reason? ... [However,] in every
> system of morality which I have hitherto met with ... the
> author proceeds for some time in the ordinary way of reason-
> ing, and establishes the being of a God, or makes observations
> concerning human affairs; when of a sudden I am surpriz'd to
> find that, instead of ... *Is,* and *Is not,* I meet with ... *ought,*
> or an *ought not* ... This *ought,* or *ought not* ... should be
> observ'd and explain'd ... A reason should be given ... how
> this new relation can be a deduction from others, which are
> entirely different from it.
>
> David Hume, *A Treatise of Human Na-
> ture,* III, I, 1.

TURNER: If I were a meta-physician and you came to me for advice, I would
prescribe this passage from Hume for reading, and direct that you meditate
on it several times a week. For in our preceding discussion you seemed to be
doing, in a covert and subtle fashion, just the sort of thing that Hume[1]
exposes here – jumping without warning or warrant from an "is" or factual
state of affairs to the production of an "ought" or moral ideal. For you
derived our ideas of moral good primarily from a certain hierarchy of attractions, and thus, if "moral good" means an "ought," you inferred our
"oughts" from these quite *factual* attractions. You can't do that. An attraction, howsoever noble or sublimated, is just a fact, albeit a psychic fact. You
can't squeeze a "thou shalt" out of a noble feeling that an individual has,
or even that most or all individuals have. Such feelings may indeed be the
source of value judgements about good and bad, as you intimate. But by
what right can you ascribe the force of an "ought" to them?

CRANSTON: You seem to be saying that I "ought" not to do this, but I
won't try to evade your question by asking how you derive *that* "ought" ...
Come now, Turner, you've read that section from Hume carefully, and I'm
sure you recall the pertinent example he gives there of the prohibition against
murder. When we say "one ought not to commit murder," according to

Hume this is an observation based merely on the strong *feeling* of disapproval or disgust we have when we contemplate such an action. In effect, we *are* deriving our moral laws from such psychological "facts." Hume does not object to deriving "oughts" from psychic facts, (because he does this himself), but only criticizes those who talk as if they are deriving "oughts" from external or *"objective"* factual states of affairs.

TURNER: I can see how you might be easily misled by that example of murder, which Hume uses. You've got some good company. Some distinguished students of Hume have been similarly misled. But you're mistaken about there being some kind of "derivation" here. Hume does not say that we *derive* "murder is wrong" from our psychic reactions against murder, but only that "murder is wrong" means "I feel a subjective abhorrence for murder." It would be silly to try to conduct a truly logical derivation here, since, for one thing, there seem to be a lot of people who are *not* troubled by such feelings of abhorrence.

CRANSTON: I agree that there is no deduction[2] involved, but there is a species of induction.[3] Hume starts with the "matter of fact" that we have a feeling of repulsion for acts of murder, a feeling which is so strong and widespread that we may reasonably doubt that any man, even the inveterate murderer, can completely extinguish it. And he generalizes, quite justifiably, that this is a basic moral imperative derived inductively from a consensus in human experience.

TURNER: He doesn't *say* all of this. And he certainly wouldn't attach much importance to this "inductive" process, even if he admitted that it prevailed. Hume had a very low opinion of logical induction as a means of arriving at truth or sound rational conclusions.[4]

CRANSTON: All right. But those of us who have a higher opinion of induction than Hume may with good reason attach a higher significance to this Humean analysis of moral judgements than Hume attached to it himself.

TURNER: I think *I* have a higher opinion of induction than Hume had. But I fail to see how this reputed emergence of "oughts" out of moral "sentiments" constitutes an induction in any real way.

CRANSTON: Let's use Hume's example: If I imagine myself murdering someone, I feel a strong reaction or repulsion. This happens a significant number of times. I generalize (by induction) that the act of murdering would be repugnant to my nature. I observe that others seem to react the same way, and I receive second-hand accounts of their experiences of repugnance, which are similar in all essential respects to my own. I finally conclude, again inductively, that there is something basically repugnant to human nature in the act of murdering. On this basis I feel justified in saying "murder is wrong," or "one *ought not* to murder." In a similar way, I and others I observe or communicate with notice that we have a positive and ennobling reaction when we imagine ourselves saving and preserving life – assuming that the capacity for, and will to, life is there (I don't want to get into the abortion controversy or the problem of euthanasia here) – and we say "one *ought* to respect and preserve life."

TURNER: It is fortunate that you and your colleagues don't happen to be sadists, and that you have obviously conducted your experiments with the imagination at a time when you were not "angry enough to kill" someone. Otherwise, I'm afraid your "induction" wouldn't get off the ground, so to speak.

CRANSTON: I am not dismayed by these countervailing examples. An induction like this merely states that there is a high probability that, because of the frequency and intensity of experiences like these, the moral judgements we form regarding respect for life or its opposite are fundamental or natural for man.

TURNER: "Natural." *Now* I see where we are drifting, and I don't like the looks of the rocks and current ahead of us. You're not using your induction to conclude, "I and most people agree that homicide is repugnant and probably bad for the murderer as well as his victim, so it would be best to refrain from it" (I would take this to be the implied content of "murder is wrong"). Rather, you are concluding that this sampling of experience by you and your confederates gives you the right to go far beyond Hume and say "there is something about the act of homicide which is basically repugnant to human *nature*." And, of course, you would take this "nature" to be some sort of stable entity, sporting certain essential features such as an instinctive respect for life or repugnance for homicide.

CRANSTON: I don't think it is necessary to bring in "nature" at all, if that term is repugnant to you. Take an example from physics: We learn by induction from our experiences with water that it boils at 100°C., so we say that is a "characteristic" of water. One fine day we heat something we thought was water to 100° C, and it doesn't boil. After painstaking investigation or chemical analysis, we discover that it wasn't pure water, but contained an admixture or solute which raised the boiling point. So our original induction stands unscathed. In like manner, we discover by appropriate inductive experiences that human beings, when they are in an optimum psychic state, find homicide repugnant, and we conclude that homicide is not an appropriate activity for such beings, i.e. it is wrong. One day we begin to notice exceptions to our generalization, and we begin to investigate these.

In one case, we find that the repugnance was there in the beginning, but was stifled by an inordinate greed (which we also consider "wrong.") In another case, we determine that an early exposure to extreme pressure from unwholesome elements in society, precluded the possibility that the repugnance could ever make itself felt (it would have to remain subconscious). In yet another, we find that an individual was so provoked by wanton acts of violence or threats or fears that he lost the repugnance he had felt ... and so on. There is nothing here to lead us to revise our original generalization that repugnance for homicide is characteristically human.

TURNER: The basic "repugnance" here seems to be a repugnance for revising or shelving our theories and generalizations ... I'm sorry, but your generalization flies in the face of the facts. You and your select coteries of fellow-introspectors may come to a fine consensus about certain repugnances characteristic to man, but if you widen your horizons a little bit both spatially and temporally, you will find that homicide is and always has been so prevalent in almost every major race and culture that an honest observer would tend to conclude that it was not only not repugnant, but conformable and even endemic, to human existence. Are you going to maintain that all of these countless counter-instances can be explained away, because you have some kind of vision of human nature in its purity, which you would rather trust than history or news reports? When there are *too* many exceptions, the rule begins to look silly, whether in physics or ethics. The very fact that there have been so many wars, in which so many obedient soldiers have apparently gone headlong into killing with pride and even gusto, and no apparent remorse, must be taken as an absolute counter-instance for the generalization you're trying to make.

CRANSTON: Soldiers in wartime hardly provide good "laboratory conditions" of human behavior. I admit that the task of isolating stress-inducing factors and other variables becomes more complicated when it comes to man. I would be the last to deny the greater complexity of human subjects as compared with any of the various and sundry objects subjected to the purview of the natural sciences. I also *admit* that the results of our generalizations, after trying to isolate pertinent variables, will boast less "certainty," which here means a lesser degree of probability,[5] than in other sciences. But the generalizations can and must be made, and the results are not invalid or untrustworthy.

TURNER: Seeing that you have just donned the garb of the "scientific" ethician, I must ask you: would you consider *me* a normal subject for your investigation.

CRANSTON: I am pleased to say that I would consider you an excellent subject.

TURNER: You will not be so pleased when you begin to examine "in depth" and record my innermost sentiments.

CRANSTON: I trust you're not a psychopath . . . ?

TURNER: No, I'm quite sane, really, and I must admit that, except at moments of extreme duress . . .

CRANSTON: You do have a temper at such moments.

TURNER: Yes. But, except during those outbreaks, which (I'm sure you will agree) are rather rare, I must admit that I feel a repugnance for the idea of homicide.

CRANSTON: You see?

TURNER: But that doesn't mean I feel any moral prohibition, or *"ought not."*

CRANSTON: That's obviously self-contradictory, because . . .

TURNER: Not at all. By the very conditions you've set up in your "laboratory experiment," I am not subject to any stresses, demeaning hostilities or prejudices at the time I am asked to entertain the idea of homicide. It goes without saying that I will, then, be basically contented and well-disposed to, if not sanguine about, the "world." There's not even the hint of a temptation to kill anyone. So an "ought" or a moral law contravening homicide would be superfluous and useless *in this situation.* Just "doing what comes naturally," I will refrain from homicide at such a time simply because of my benevolent and eudaemonic feelings and my unwillingness to disturb them in the least. So now, what happens to your "induction"?

CRANSTON: You've come up with a Kantian objection, and I think it is a weighty one. There can be no "ought" in the absence of conflict or stress. Kant had in mind the conflict between the inclinations and "reason." I do not think it is necessary for *us* to draw up the battle lines in precisely that way, but nevertheless Kant was on the right track. It is only when there is some kind of internal conflict or stress that the feeling that gives rise to "ought" and the idea of moral "duties" and "obligations" really emerges. So I would have to qualify my previous statement about "isolating variables."[6] And so (getting back to the case of the taboo against homicide) there would have to be at least some stress or hostility or prejudice inducing a tug-of-war between one's respect for life and his anger or temptation to take a life, for our study to be relevant. But there should be no overwhelming contravening factors, such as would tend to obliterate all semblance of the struggle. The struggle must remain, and perdure during the course of our observations.

TURNER: The conditions you are setting up seem practically impossible to achieve, but I suppose they might be theoretically possible to obtain. I will accept them. Let us suppose that at some time in one of my more un-guarded moments I happen to be in the precise psychic homeostasis of con-flict that you consider prerequisite to conducting your observations of the emergence of morality from my psyche. Now, in line with your previous remarks, I suppose you would say that my attraction or sentiment for respecting and preserving life generates the "ought" here, while my relatively less attraction, i.e. repugnance, for taking human life generates the pertinent and corresponding "ought not."

CRANSTON: I think it should be stated more precisely than that. The "ought" consists of a feeling of attraction which is intermingled with a simultaneous ambivalent but subordinate repugnance for the *same object* – in this case, "reverence for life." If a person, feeling this pro-life sentiment, did not have at least some misgivings or ambivalence about it, it would not, strictly speaking, be an "ought" at all, but a pure feeling providing an ap-proximation to what Kant calls the "holy will." In a similar fashion, "ought not" here, which emphasizes a repugnance for taking life, would have to be intermingled with a simultaneous attraction of some sort for that *same object* – otherwise the "ought not" would be unnecessary and, indeed, un-intelligible.

TURNER: What you say seems to jibe, in general, with my experience. But alas, there is not necessarily *any* relationship of this "conflict" you are adum-brating, to what we call "morality." A cannibal, for instance, could feel himself in the throes of an "ought" as he tries to decide whether to eat a captured enemy now or save his carcass for the big celebration of his son's circumcision coming up in a week. A "hit man" could be plagued by the proddings of conscience as he prepares to murder someone who happened to do a kindness for him in the past: but "conscience," for the "hit man," means only that he considers using more humane and risky methods of eliminating his victim rather than swift and less detectable, but crueler, methods. I don't think I need to multiply examples any further. These are not what we would call "moral" decisions.

CRANSTON: No. Not what *we* would call "moral." But this, of course, suggests that we have to be selective about the types of conflict we consider to be relevant to morality. We must define the basic opposition that *we* (normal, civilized people) consider to be essential to the dynamics of moral-ity.

TURNER: Which is?

CRANSTON: I think the most basic moral opposition is the opposition or tension between the empirical and ideal self.[7] I don't mean anything mys-terious and metaphysical by this. Freud expresses the opposition quite well when in his later writings he describes the conflict between the ego and the super-ego (or ego-ideal). Behavioral psychologists speak of the relationship between the self-concept and the "level of aspiration" – a kind of ideal goal that an individual sets for himself.

TURNER: Your interpretation of these categorizations sounds more existential than psychological.

CRANSTON: I don't deny that. In Kierkegaard's existentialism, for example, the dynamic relationship between the "real" and the "ideal" self is considered essential to the ethical "sphere."[8] But I would say that the findings of psychology seem to offer scientific corroboration for that "existential" insight. I could mention other psychologists who found it necessary to use similar explanatory constructs – William James, Carl Jung, Rollo May ...

TURNER: That's not necessary. All you really seem to be saying is that everyone who is not just vegetating sets up ideals or goals for himself. I'm not going to make a big issue out of an assertion like that. But when all is said and done, the conflict you have set up is anticlimactic. It's hardly related to morality at all. My ideal, or "ideal self" as you prefer to call it, could be quite trivial. My whole purpose in life could be to look like and imitate Humphrey Bogart. How many moral points or credits do I get for that? Or it could even be something perverted, like getting international press coverage by assassinating the President of the United States. I should imagine one would even get quite a few demerits for having an ideal like that.

CRANSTON: No, no. It has to be something serious – a serious ideal. And it has to be something that emerges from the individual himself, his own ideal, free from the vestiges of outside influences or suggestions.

TURNER: I have never found it easy to accept the concept of "virgin birth" – no matter from what source. The notion of someone giving birth to ideals or goals completely free from external influences seems like a "virgin birth" to be ... something completely miraculous, and definitely beyond my powers of comprehension.

CRANSTON: I appreciate your sense of humor, Turner, but I don't think the comical spirit is the best disposition for getting a "handle" on this problem. I'm not saying one's personal ideal is produced *in vitro* or on some rarified Olympian heights, but only that its source must be veridically spontaneous – from within. The ideal must be your *own* ideal, your own creation. You may have received all sorts of stimuli towards the ideal from without. The selective depth reaction to these stimuli is what *you* contribute.

TURNER: Who is to say what is a serious and creative ideal, and what is not?

CRANSTON: There's one ideal that I consider to be self-evidently serious and obviously the result of creative reflection: the ideal of overcoming alienation or conflict *itself* – i.e. all of these conflicts between opposing attractions which disturb the psyche, whether the conflicts in question are moral, amoral or immoral.[9]

TURNER: A short time ago you began with what I guess we could call a "first-order" statement about the function of conflicts in inducing an ethical attitude. And now since you have been unable to satisfactorily distinguish "moral" conflicts from the non-moral, you make a sudden and unscheduled retreat to a "second-order" conflict, the conflict between the factual state of (first-order) conflict and the ideal of overcoming it.

CRANSTON: I would express it differently: as the conflict between 1) the desire for overcoming conflict and 2) the opposite desire for remaining in the state of conflict.

TURNER: The "desire to overcome conflict" may be simply a manifestation of the desire to escape (psychic) pain. The "desire to remain in the state of conflict" is very probably just a case of psychic inertia, laziness. Do you really think you have the makings of a psychological-moral drama here?

CRANSTON: Actually, the words "overcome" and "remain in" may be misleading. "To overcome conflict" here means to *transcend* conflict by attaining a kind of constructive equilibrium or equipoise between the conflicting elements. "To remain in conflict" means to recognize a certain dynamic tension within one's personality as a necessary pre-condition for personal moral progress and to *perpetuate* that tension with this in mind. As you can see, it's altogether a somewhat paradoxical psychic state to be in.

TURNER: Paradoxical indeed! I suppose at this juncture I would be justified in throwing my hands up in confusion and making my exit, but in a conciliatory frame of mind and with due regard to the bonds of friendship I will try to render what you are saying logically coherent in a basic sort of way. Let us call the former conflict between various attractions and repulsions Alienation$_1$. Then this conflict now between the desire to perpetuate and the desire to transcend Alienation$_1$ becomes a second-order Alienation, or Alienation$_2$. Is that right?

CRANSTON: You could express it in those terms. But before you succumb to the impulse to "puncture my baloon," let me try to clarify my assertion: All I'm saying is that the essential ethical imperative for man is to maintain a creative constructive and dynamic opposition between the present Alienations$_1$ that he is conscious of, and the ideal of overcoming these Alienations$_1$. If the "ought" or ideal in this case is insufficiently different from the way he actually is, the opposition will be innocuous and non-dynamic. If the ideal is too lofty and unattainable, again a static and stagnant state will result. Only if the ideal is set up at a realistic distance from one's empirical state, and with an artful and creative view to one's own needs and one's own responses to his environment, will the proper "dynamic" be established – a dynamic which invites itself to be overcome, so to speak. But the overcoming of the opposition entailed by this dynamic will not, optimally, lead to mere cessation of conscious activity, but to the production of a new creative opposition. The constant oscillation between the skillful perpetuation of this opposition and its resolution through attainment of the ideals proposed or projected, is synonymous with what we call the moral life.

TURNER: I'll try again: To remain moral one must in a sense be alienated. Don't you find something intuitively dissatisfying about that idea?

CRANSTON: There are alienations and there are alienations. As I've explained, this is a constructive alienation, and quite beneficial to the personality. However, if the very idea of perpetuating an alienation seems troublesome, there are other options. As I think we agreed in our discussion of good and evil, the moral good and moral existence could conceivably be superseded or forestalled by other species of good – for example, religious or aesthetic experience.

TURNER: Don't you suspect that if you subjected these other levels of existence to analysis, you might find some species of alienation in them, too.

CRANSTON: No, I don't think so.

TURNER: I'll leave that "sleeping dog" rest for now. Getting back to the problem Hume proposed: I take it that you will no longer insist that the "ought" is derived from attractions, or what Hume called sentiments of approbation; or from the simple conflict of attractions with their simple opposites. You would now like to say the "ought" can be "derived" from Alienation$_2$ as a kind of fact. Is that correct?

CRANSTON: Alienation$_2$ as I have described it is a fact of *moral* existence. If you have existed on the moral level at all, you know what it means to project, and progressively approximate to, life-goals. I'm sure you have experienced this as a fact of your own existence.

TURNER: In all honesty I must say that I think anyone who supposes he has experienced this Alienation$_2$ has been reading existentialist[10] writings or Kant's[11] moral treatises, or has in someway been brainwashed into thinking that this caterpillar-like enterprise of catching up with one's "true (non-alienated) self" is the distilled essence of a rich and rewarding, if melancholy, life. When one is fully equipped with these less than rose-colored metaphysical glasses, it is hardly wondrous that he just happens to "find" the fact of Alienation$_2$ staring him in the face with everything he does.

CRANSTON: What I'm talking about doesn't need to be a constant state.

Do you mean to tell me that you've never sat down and tried to determine where you're going in life, whether your goals and the means of attaining them are viable, and how you might further your personal progress (without, however, trying to completely escape the conflicts which brought you to this state of meditation in the first place)?

TURNER: Cranston, I don't want to shock you, so prepare yourself: No, I have to say that I've never sat down to do anything quite like that. And yet, for all that, I would like to insist that I'm a basically moral person.

CRANSTON: You must have done this implicitly and instinctively, without actually reflecting on what you were doing.

TURNER: Perhaps. But even so, you would not be able to salvage your argument. It's clear that you want very much to say that Alienation$_2$ is some kind of second-order fact of experience from which the moral "ought" can be immediately and intuitively induced or "derived." But, in addition to this second-order *fact*, you now have a second-order *"ought"*; because it's not the ordinary run-of-the-mill "oughts" that you're interested in, but this special, unique "ought" which you equate with Alienation$_2$, the "ought" of overcoming Alienation$_1$. In short, the whole distinction between "fact" and moral idea or value, which was originally there, has been obliterated, so that it doesn't make any sense to "derive" the one from the other.

CRANSTON: I can see what you mean. It would be meaningless to "derive" B from A if both A and B are qualified or added to in such a way that the meaning of each begins to converge with the other on a higher level.

TURNER: I'm not sure about calling it a "higher" level. But that's the general idea.

CRANSTON: But *you* have "oughts," Turner. I am taking for granted that you have at least first-order "oughts." Doesn't it bother you that the source of these oughts is unknown – that they seem to appear "out of the blue" and with insufficient justification? In other words, that they are "un-derived" elements of your psyche.

TURNER: I'm sorry. That really doesn't bother me. And I'm beginning to see that the problem in our discussion all along has really been in the way you have portrayed the "ought." You seem to look upon it as some kind of hallowed prescription for behavior, which man had better follow or else face the consequences of shallowness, meaninglessness, and spiritual disintegration. If you formulate it in this fashion, then of course you are burdened with the task of explaining how such a mysterious entity ever emerged out of the workaday world. But if you demystify it as Hume actually did, and see it as just a covert way of saying, "I really like this style of behavior," or "I want to do this, although I'm also attracted to other contrary courses of action" (a formulation which you might prefer) – the problem disappears. I don't need to dig deep for some "source" from which expressions like this are supposedly derived.

CRANSTON: But you need to explain the sense of obligation which is associated with such statements.

TURNER: I have no such need, because I don't construe "obligation" the way you do, as if it were some norm imposed on man from on high, regardless of the satisfaction he attains or forfeits in adhering to these obligations. There is no such thing, and there is no way of proving that even the most universally acknowledged moral norms, such as "don't murder" are intrinsically true or valid or justified. If we dislike and want to discourage such things as murder, we would best use our energy in formulating positive and constructive counter-incentives to that act, and an appropriate apparatus of punishments to deal with offenders, rather than inscribing the stone tablets and embellishing the archways of our life with impressively designed and mysterious-looking "thou shalts" or "thou shalt not's."

CHAPTER III

VIRTUE AND TEMPERAMENT

> In the moral part of the soul there are two types of virtue, natural virtue and virtue in the strict sense ... The same man ... is not best equipped by nature for all the virtues ...
>
> Aristotle, *Nichomachean Ethics*, VI, 13

> From the side of the body, according to the nature of each individual there are certain habitual tendencies which provide natural beginnings for virtue. For some people by their temperament are well disposed toward chastity, others to a "good temper," and so forth.
>
> Thomas Aquinas, *Summa Theologiae* I–II, 51–1

CRANSTON: In our previous discussion, we were discussing Alienation$_1$, or the type of psychic conflict which seems to give rise to the experience of the "ought." In regard to that experience, you pointed out the difficulty of determining whether the "ought" that was generated would be what we call "moral" or not. You gave the examples of the sort of "ought" that a cannibal or a "hit man" might feel. And, in response to that objection, I suggested that the concept of Alienation$_2$ might provide a criterion for determining whether an "ought" was "serious" or not. You had some difficulty accepting this criterion, so perhaps another approach is called for: It occurs to me that a somewhat modified version of the ancient and mediaeval distinction between "natural" and "acquired" virtue might help to further clarify just when an "ought" is serious and strictly moral, and when not.

TURNER: I don't see any immediate relevance of this distinction to the issue at hand, but I'm open to suggestions.

CRANSTON: By "natural virtue" I have in mind what is now generally referred to in psychological circles as "temperament." The contemporary equivalent to "acquired virtue" would be the psychological concept of "character" (which generally implies something achieved or acquired by effort, rather than innate or inborn); or perhaps our simple term, "virtue," without any qualification, would do the trick, since it generally connotes something acquired by effort.

TURNER: The word "virtue" now, when used without qualification in popular parlance, almost always has the connotation of "chastity."

CRANSTON: This is no formidable objection against our use of the word. We've been using the term, "moral," so far, without any qualms or hesitation. But when you see "moral" or "morals" used without qualification in the newspapers or elsewhere, sexual morality is almost always meant.

TURNER: That's a strange phenomenon, isn't it? I suppose Freud may have an explanation for it. At any rate, your point is well taken: If philosophers can discuss "morality" and "immorality" without being taken in by the vagaries of the *lingua franca*, I guess we can do the same thing with "virtue." However, when "virtue" is used in a kind of Platonic/Aristotelian sense,[1] it implies the existence of an independent substantial soul and various kinds of non-sensory "faculties." And I find this implication overly metaphysical and indeed superfluous.

CRANSTON: I think it is quite possible to utilize this concept without any necessary reference to ancient theories about inner potentialities or faculties.[2] All *we* are going to imply by the term is the possession of moral qualities by a personality or psyche. We can suspend judgement as to whether the personality has distinct faculties or is a mere "stream of consciousness" in William James' sense.

TURNER: I don't want to be a stickler for semantics, but I have problems with the term, "temperament." When I hear that term, I recall the "four temperaments" of Hippocrates and Galen[3] and all the old theories about black and yellow "humors" in the body and the effect they're supposed to have on people's behavior. I know the word, "temperament" still pops up now and then, even in psychological literature, but it definitely seems to be on the way out.

CRANSTON: I think what you are objecting to primarily is the attempt to correlate the various temperaments with corresponding bodily dispositions or body types. But a lot of work has been done on this since the "humor" theory of medicine became passé. In our own century, Kretschmer and Sheldon have had a great influence on medicine and sociology as well as psychology by their theories concerning the correlation of body types and temperaments.

TURNER: You misunderstand the nature of *my* objection. I do not have any particular difficulty appreciating the efforts of scientists to correlate physical and psychological factors. I'm not aware of any spectacular successes in this area as of this date, but to me the endeavor seems worthwhile: why *not* look to physical factors for the clues to personality traits, etc.? If they ever come up with some proofs, I'll be open to accepting them. So that's not my objection. The thing I don't like is the use that is made of the "types" or categories that result. Maybe there are some pyknics and asthenics[4] running around, but if we use these Kretschmerian classifications to predict the behavior and reactions of people, and put them into a "mold," the whole enterprise is an insult to human empathy.

CRANSTON: William Sheldon[5] tried to avoid the sort of stereotyping you object to by developing clusters of traits which allow a lot of room for individual variations: He tried to show that each of the twenty "viscerotonic" traits correlates positively with all the others, and negatively with twenty "somatotonic" and twenty "cerebrotonic" traits. Even if one happened to turn out as a "viscerotonic," a very large number of variations are possible depending on an individual's rating on the sixty traits that contribute to one's psychological "profile."

TURNER: That's no doubt a step in the right direction. But I don't like the idea of classifying people, even by "clusters of variables." There may be something to this concept, "temperament"; but psychological research indicates that "temperament" itself is the result of a lot of conditioning by the environment, not of some innate or intrinsic tendency which comes from my heredity, bodily makeup, or even the clusters of traits that one happened to have yesterday when he was typed by a Sheldonian psychologist.

CRANSTON: I don't think we have to determine at this point *what* the origin or cause of a "temperamental disposition" might be. It *may be* caused wholly or largely by external factors, as you maintain. However, I might just mention that, according to Sheldon, this *expectation* of people that personality is determined from without rather than from within, would itself be a "non-cerebrotonic" characteristic.

TURNER: So – modern psychologists are not generally cerebrotonics. I'm sure they would experience difficulty in comprehending Alienation$_2$!... But back to the present problem: How does all this business about temperament throw any further light on the "ought," anyway?

CRANSTON: To recapitulate: We agreed on the necessity of Alienation$_1$, i.e. some sort of conflict between inclinations or attractions, to explain the experience of an "ought." But we were unable to distinguish adequately a moral conflict and a moral "ought," from their immoral or amoral counterparts. But now, if we allow that a temperamental disposition could give us a major and powerful impulse or orientation to act in one way rather than another, a useful distinction can be made between what I might call the temperamental "ought" (T-ought) and the moral "ought" (M-ought). Both "oughts" result from a conflict or Alienation$_1$. But the T-ought results from the conflict of *a)* a powerful temperamental predisposition with *b)* external or internal obstacles to acting in accord with that disposition. If we could put the T-ought into words, it would read something like this: I *ought* to fulfill this impulse which is a major demand of my being and shows promise of providing happiness to me, but I am experiencing such-and-such impediments which have the potential for preventing or delaying this fulfillment. The M-ought, on the other hand, is best exemplified when a major temperamental disposition is itself counteracted by an act of the will instigated by a sense of duty. The conflict, in this case, is often depicted in common speech as "doing violence to oneself," or some similar phraseology.

Now, the examples of the cannibal and the "hit man" which you used in our previous discussion were both T-oughts: the tremendous satisfaction which the cannibal was accustomed to deriving from his cannibalism could be taken as just a perverted habit like alcoholism, or like the sensual delinquencies that Aristotle referred to as "incontinence," in which case there would hardly be any "ought." But it might also be taken as a kind of command deriving from one's very psychological makeup, and the particular needs essential to the happiness of this individual. Let us hypothesize that the cannibal embodies what Sheldon calls the "viscerotonic" temperament. One of the primary traits associated with this temperament is the fact that the act of eating has a strong ritual and almost religious significance for a person of this temperament. For a cannibal with such a temperament, the act of eating another human being could be associated with the very pinnacle of religious sentiment connected with eating; and to refuse to engage in it, on a particular occasion, would be seriously frustrating. In regard to the "hit man," let us suppose that he is a "somatotonic." One of the primary traits of a somatotonic is an unusual aggressivity, combined with a need to prove one's dominance and courage. It can easily be seen that, for *such* a temperament, to forfeit on making the prescribed "hit" might amount to an act of cowardice. As an illustration of the M-ought, on the other hand, one of Kant's examples may help: the cold-hearted individual who has little natural sympathy for others, and is weighed down by sorrows, but nevertheless engages in philanthropy out of a moral regard for others. In Sheldon's terms, this would be the introverted "cerebrotonic.' type, who manages to *overcome* his natural antisocial proclivities. Sheldon would call such an individual a "sublimated" cerebrotonic.

TURNER: It's convenient for you that you chose that particular example, because I can think of some other examples of "contrary" inclinations which might not fit so easily into any of Sheldon's categories. For instance, let us say that both an extreme cerebrotonic and an extreme somatotonic commit suicide. Since the cerebrotonic is predisposed to be cowardly and has a natural fear of death, I suppose the act of suicide would be virtuous for him (an M-ought); while the same act would be less virtuous or even a T-ought for the naturally courageous somatotonic.

CRANSTON: I'm not ruling out the possibility that the act of suicide could be virtuous in some cases, but one would have to know an awful lot about the motives to make a judgement like this. The motives for suicide could range from fear of living to a desire to retaliate against friends or family to a need to prove one's manhood in a dramatic act. It all depends. All I can say is that if we could show that a man has chosen a line of behavior which runs counter to his major temperamental inclinations, we would have a good example of an M-ought. I don't deny that it may be difficult to determine what his major inclinations are and/or what his real motives for acting are.

TURNER: It's significant that you chose Kant as your authority on the "M-ought." Your whole idea of morality seems to hinge on the negation of the inclinations, an idea which was so dear to Kant.

CRANSTON: Why describe the "M-ought" as a negation? It's a case where the will as a positive force supersedes strong inclinations to which we are disposed by temperament.

TURNER: On your line of thought, the masochist[6] who feels he has to punish himself severely twice a day just to "keep in shape," would be the epitome of the M-ought.

CRANSTON: Here again, one would have to know a lot about the intentions of the masochist and his major temperamental inclinations to make a valid judgement. But I would say that, taking a *prima facie* look at the situation, the masochistic acts seem to be an example of the T-ought. The somatotonic temperament, for instance is well adapted to the unflinching endurance of pain and towards boasting about "battle scars" of all sorts. If a somatotonic became masochistic, this could best be interpreted as the result of a T-ought.

TURNER: I should think it would be possible for you or for anyone pre-judiced in favor of the M-ought, to interpret almost any action they dis-approved of as a T-ought. Even acts of supreme self-sacrifice could be inter-preted as latent but definitely self-serving masochism.

CRANSTON: No, I don't think that's true. There are certain paradigmatic cases which it would be almost impossible to interpret as T-oughts. For example, the act of sacrificing one's life or happiness for others. One could hardly have a selfish or egoistic motive in performing such actions.

TURNER: I think you are underestimating the difficulty of determining whether specific actions are altruistic, or not. For example, Erich Fromm says that there is a type of person who is so neurotically selfless and in-cessantly "giving," that he or she becomes an intolerable burden to everybody ... But I need not marshall this sort of neo-Freudianism on my behalf, because I can argue this point on your own grounds – old-fashioned temperament. Let us say that your "unselfish person" who sacrifices his life for others believes that he will be rewarded in an afterlife for his action. Isn't there a Sheldonian temperament-type characterized by greed? I think *I* would be justified in interpreting all this self-sacrifice as a very rare and admittedly sublimated manifestation of greed for a heavenly reward. Or let us suppose that our heroic individual is irreligious. I could simply interpret his act of sacrificing his life as a species of concupiscence, a hankering after the peace and quiet of the eternal oblivion that he thinks he is going to enjoy when he dies.

CRANSTON: I seem to be handicapped, as in our previous discussion, by our lack of a common pool of experience in these matters. It's a definite impediment to communication. What am I to say if you simply deny that reason and will can supersede temperamental inclinations in a positive and non-morbid way? If you really believe that all of your behavior is explainable in terms of one or the other "inclination" coming to the fore, how could you be expected to recognize and admit that this or that instance of behavior is unexplainable in terms of "purely natural" inclinations?

TURNER: You're giving up too soon. We're not really at an impasse – not yet. In fact, I am now in a position to offer you an "olive branch" which you won't be able to refuse. (At least I don't think you will be able to.) It's a true instance of dialectic; a dialectical solution to our apparently divergent moral experiences. I propose that we forget about T-oughts and M-oughts, and recognize the fact (which is being forced upon us by this discussion) that there are really two different types of *M-oughts* – first of all the HM-ought, or the "ought" which is oriented to the pursuit of basic and essential happiness, or what you might call temperamental imperatives; and secondly, the DM-ought, or the "ought" which is oriented towards counteracting inclinations in the name of "duty" – an "ought" which you and many of the cerebrotonic-melancholic temperament seem to have vivid experiences of. And so, in line with this distinction, you in observing a moral action would tend to describe it as a checking or restraint of basic impulses, while I, observing the same action, might characterize it as a "sublimated"[7] manifestation of impulses or passions. I'm emphasizing happiness like a good utilitarian and you're emphasizing duty like a loyal Kantian, but we both agree that the action is moral, a moral "ought." What do you think of my peace initiative?

CRANSTON: Since you don't offer such initiatives lightly or frequently, I don't want to seem indifferent or unresponsive to this one, especially since it evinces an interesting dialectic. But still, I'm afraid this HM-ought of yours has some serious and perhaps fatal flaws. When you concede that a moral act according to the HM-ought would have to be interpreted as a "*sublimation*" of some inclination – that's obviously a euphemism for the "rational restraint of inclination," and you are giving implicit recognition to the fact that we have a *duty* to sublimate inclinations. But you phrase your statements in such a way as to present a duty-ethic in the guise of a happiness-ethic.

TURNER: I think we are having some problems about the connotation of "sublimation." "Sublimation" to my mind simply means letting some of the finer and more representative emotions or inclinations come to the fore at the right time and in the right circumstances. I can't for the life of me understand why you insist on incorporating negation and restriction into your concept of the M-ought. Why all this talk about "overcoming tendencies"? Why not talk instead about capitalizing on the positive tendencies, assets, strong points, or talents in one's psychological makeup?

CRANSTON: Your use of the word, "capitalize," is significant and symbolic here. The positive qualities that one possesses as a result of his temperament, are a kind of "capital" that one starts off with in his life or activity. I won't try to specify whether this "capital" is the result of inheritance or of some lucky accidents befalling one in one's environment – we agreed not to make an issue of this. The main point is – the fact that we are endowed with this "capital" is not due to any special effort or *merit* on our part. We can hardly make a virtue out of such endowments, unless you want to allow that they have been acquired through efforts of the will – in which case you are getting into a DM-ought rather than what you would like to call an HM-ought.

TURNER: You just can't seem to brook the idea of people following their inclinations, pursuing happiness, and doing a hell of a lot of good for others as well as themselves in the long run. You are never going to sanctify such activity by calling it "moral," are you? You don't seem to realize that "reason," as you call it, can best be put to use by fostering and channeling one's positive qualities. If this were done, the base or negative qualities that you are so worried about would scarcely have a chance to rear their ugly heads, and we would not have to busy ourselves with "negating" them.

CRANSTON: I repeat, I am fully in favor of fostering and perpetuating one's positive and constructive desires and inclinations. But this comes under the rubric of the "right of self-fulfillment," not of "morality" in the strict sense. In fact, what you are really talking about are *rights*, not duties. Human beings have all kinds of rights, many of which are no doubt rooted in very fundamental inclinations. But these rights are not moral "oughts." For example, I have a right to life and liberty, to recognition, to fair treatment. But it would not even be good English usage for me to characterize these rights as "moral obligations." The concept of "moral obligation" here creeps up only with regard to the duty of *others* to respect my right for life, to treat me fairly, etc. And thus, while I am all in favor of temperamental imperatives, and even consider myself under a moral obligation (or DM-ought) to respect those imperatives in others, it would be ambiguous and misleading for me to speak of these imperatives as a *moral* "ought" of any sort.

TURNER: In line with this sort of reasoning, you would have to maintain, if you are consistent, that utilitarianism is not a form of ethics at all. For utilitarianism in all of its formulations is geared to the pursuit of happiness. And you would like to say that in choosing means to the attainment of happiness, we are actually just making calculations concerning the most prudent ways of achieving our rights, rather than fulfilling our moral obligations in any way, shape or form. Or do I interpret you correctly?

CRANSTON: You interpretation would be valid only for the extremely egoistic brand of utilitarianism.[8] But as you know, most presently prevailing forms of utilitarianism insist that the happiness of others must be placed on at least an equal par with one's own happiness. In other words, there is this widely recognized but still largely unexplained leap from the pursuit of one's own happiness to concern for that of others. If one possess this latter concern to the extent of being willing to sacrifice his own happiness to promote the happiness of others, he seems to me to have definitely gone beyond the parameters of rights and fulfillment to duty and morality.

TURNER: I suppose you are within your "rights" in bringing up this matter of a person "sacrificing" his own happiness in favor of another's happiness. But, as I indicated earlier, I think it would be almost impossible to *prove* that this is actually what takes place in any given instance of individual altruism or heroism. And so I think I have the duty of advising you that . . .

CRANSTON: It's not necessary. I can see your point. But I just hope you yourself realize the implications of what you are saying. If utilitarianism has not and cannot get beyond egoism even in its devotion to the "greatest happiness of the greatest number," it is better characterized as a calculus for the attainment of personal rights than as a code of morality.

TURNER: Quite so, if one follows your extremely strict "ground rules" according to which a scrupulous and stark distinction between "rights" and "duties" must always be maintained. But thankfully, in real life, matters are a little more relaxed, so to speak. For example, I have *both* a right *and* a duty to cultivate my talents, to work, to fulfill myself sexually, and so forth.

CRANSTON: What you have come up with here are examples of things which can be either rights or duties, depending on their context. Work is a right when it is a matter of activating my creative potentialities, but a duty when it involves a denial of some of my basic desires or propensities; the cultivation of talents is a right for those who are inclined that way, but a duty for those who, because of laziness, fear, etc. are prone to "bury" their talents; sexual fulfillment is ordinarily thought of as a natural right, but becomes a duty for extremely neurotic or misanthropic individuals whose sexual frustration causes problems not only for themselves but for others.

TURNER: It's becoming clearer and clearer: You seem to think that anything which is just a wee bit enjoyable or "in line with my temperamental inclinations" is immoral. This is not ethics but Puritanism.

CRANSTON: You misunderstand both me and the Puritans, Turner. The point is not that enjoyment is wrong, but that something done purely for the *sake* of enjoyment, or the fulfillment of inclinations, is amoral. It's only when we freely subjugate inclination to conscious intentions (i.e., *rational* attractions) that there is even the possibility of morality.

Please understand me. I'm not as morbid as you think. I am all in favor of people enjoying themselves and fostering all the positive qualities with which they are temperamentally endowed. But why call this sort of thing a matter of *morality*, unless, as I've already said, some supervening circumstance should change the context of the activity in question? Apply "Ockham's razor"[9] here: People following their own laws of psychic inertia are always going to do what they are inclined to do, unless some intervening force changes the direction or intent of their endeavors. What is to be gained by portraying the momentum of primal endeavors as "moral"? No one is claiming that they are *im*moral. They just belong in another more suitable category, the category of rights.

TURNER: I think you are drawing up the alternatives much too simplistically here: On the one hand, you say, we have a group of actions which result purely from temperamental inclinations, even temperamental inclinations of the best sort and with the highest pedigree. And these actions you would classify as "the pursuit of rights" in very diverse ways. In the opposite corner, you point out another group of actions which involve some sort of negation of major temperamental inclinations, and these you would be willing to dub "moral," provided, I presume, that the negation was dictated by certain good reasons of at least a very subjective sort.

CRANSTON: Yes, of course, that is implied. If there were not good reasons, then it would be simply a matter of one supervening whim or inclination countermanding another.

TURNER: Very well. But I would like to point out that you are leaving out a very broad third category of actions – the category which is very probably most applicable to the majority of human actions: namely, the category of actions which are done for what you would consider to be quite moral reasons, but which *also* happen to be in accord with our inclinations. Surely you admit the existence of such a category?

CRANSTON: Only in a qualified sense. Saying that an action is "in accord with our inclinations" and also "moral" in its intent is an ambivalent statement, if you examine it closely. For we could not *know* if the action was moral unless at the very minimum there were a willingness to immediately desist from the action if reason and will were to so dictate. How can one ever be *sure*, when borne on the wave of a present inclination, that he is sufficiently detached from that inclination to give it up in the name of morality?

TURNER: Then Carrie Nation and the rest of that gloomy band of famous moralists are right: if you want to make people moral, make them renounce and suffer and sacrifice. You seem to be joining your voice to theirs.

CRANSTON: No, I've already admitted that this very large class of actions that you've referred to can be moral if there is a basic willingness to renounce the actions and the inclinations which are concomitant to them, for good reasons.

I am beginning to perceive that the basic issue with regard to this third class of actions is primarily *epistemological*.[10] It's not a question of whether activity in accord with major inclinations can be moral. Sure it can. Much of it probably *is* moral. But there's no way of *knowing* for sure that it's moral. When one does something that one likes, he himself and we as observers must always suspect that he did it *because* he liked it, rather than for any moral motives. To use another example from Kant: if a tradesman has a natural like for people and a natural desire to maintain his reputation in a small town, we cannot be *sure* that his motives for charging fair prices are moral. Kant is right. If we ever want to be *sure* that we are acting morally we have to have the experience of actually going against the inclinations out of respect for duty. Here is the clear advantage of a Kantian ethic over a utilitarian ethic of the egoistic variety. Such an ethic may very well embody a high degree of moral behavior, but it can never *know* for sure that it does. Kantian morality, on the other hand, although it may have the handicap of "negativity," is nevertheless a *self-conscious* ethic: the Kantian moralist knows *that* he is moral, *why* he is moral, and *when* he is moral.

TURNER: This sounds like a declaration of war.

CRANSTON: Give me a chance to put it all together. I am willing to go along with you in admitting that for normal people the rational pursuit of happiness is an important and perhaps the most important aspect of their daily life. But it is only at times when they experience themselves counteracting natural tendencies out of a sense of duty that they can have *certainty* of their morality, i.e. attain to full moral consciousness, consciousness of the "ought." Activity that you would like to designate as a "HM-ought" *may* be an M-ought *or* merely a T-ought. In other words, we can never be sure if it is an M-ought at all. It is only the DM-oughts that we can be *sure* are M-oughts. And so, while the pursuit of happiness may be the most important thing in the conduct of life, the experience of the effort involved in adhering to duty is the most important contributing factor to the development of a moral consciousness. I think you should be able to see now that what I am saying is imbued with the spirit of compromise and easily amounts to a "peace initiative."

TURNER: I'm sure you must have had to summon up your most benign and compromising spirit in order to admit that the HM-ought may "possibly" exist; and I suspect that this admission may have even involved some effort in the strictly moral sense on your part, since you don't seem to have had any inclination to make the admission previously. However, you are mistaken in trying to place the problem on an epistemological level. The proper level for appreciating this issue is the *metaphysical* level.[11] It's not just the *knowledge* of morality that *you* are concerned with maintaining and establishing with your DM-ought, but some of your covert metaphysical presuppositions in favor of "free will."[12] You know only too well that it is only by extolling man's ability to grit his teeth and master his inclinations that you can bolster your idea of a will which is independent of physical urgings. But I can't be a party to this dichotomization of man. I told you in our last discussion that you had a tendency to mystify the "ought" and make it something sacred. For all practical purposes, it doesn't make much difference whether you achieve this mystification by pointing to some source "on high," or by referring to some power independent of matter which is supposed to exist within the deepest recesses of the soul. The effect is the same in both cases – mystification.

CRANSTON: Am I to understand that you deny human freedom? You seemed to have democratic tendencies.

TURNER: I certainly favor politico-social freedom in a kind of Hobbesian sense[13] – the right of man to pursue happiness with a minimum of restraints and obstacles from others. This idea is obviously incompatible with your notion of freedom as some kind of a pure spiritual power. In fact, I feel convinced you would have to say that the more obstacles a person meets up with in his environment, the more he can become cognizant of his freedom.

Put him in chains, and let him experience the pure ecstasy of negativistic Kantian freedom!

CRANSTON: That's a caricature of what I am saying. I only claim that a certain modicum of what you call "negative" experiences, i.e. the experiences of personal restraint and renunciation, are necessary for developing one's consciousness of personal moral freedom. I thought this was self-evident and I'm surprised to see you resisting the idea so strenuously. You must have had permissive parents!

TURNER: Yes, they put so much emphasis on my cultivating my "natural" virtues, that I don't have the faintest notion of what it is like to acquire a virtue by a sheer act of will and by invoking the combined patronage of Kant and St. Thomas Aquinas.

CRANSTON: Perhaps there are some people who experience what you call "metaphysical" freedom, and are free; and there are others who don't experience it and thus can't know what I'm talking about.

TURNER: I know you don't really believe that. You just wouldn't feel comfortable with *laissez-faire* in the area of moral experience.

CRANSTON: I don't think it is impossible that we could find some areas of broad agreement. For instance, although we have some basic differences as to the nature of subjective moral experience, I suspect that we need not be at loggerheads regarding the objective correlates of moral experience. Protestants and Catholics, communists and capitalists, even thieves and lawmen often are able to find principles and practices that they agree on. There must be some objective "common denominators" of morality that we can agree on. We actually do seem to agree on objective norms of morality in practical life. But how do you clarify or justify this agreement theoretically? What's its rationale? This is a serious question.

CHAPTER IV

SUBJECTIVE AND OBJECTIVE MORALITY

> The Superman, I have at heart; *that* is the first and only thing
> to me – and *not* man: not the neighbor, not the poorest, not the
> sorriest, not the best – ...
> Today have the petty people become master: They all preach
> submission and humility and diligence and consideration and
> the long *et cetera* of petty virtues ...
> These masters of today – surpass them, O my brethren –
> these petty people: *they* are the Superman's greatest danger! ...
> "Man must become better and eviler" – so do I teach. The
> evilest is necessary for the Superman's best.
>
> > Zarathustra in Friedrich Nietzsche's *Thus
> > Spake Zarathustra*, IV, 73

> Each of us has to find out for himself what is permitted and
> what is forbidden – forbidden for him. It's possible for one
> never to transgress a single law and still be a bastard. And
> vice versa. Actually it's only a question of convenience. Those
> who are too lazy and comfortable to think for themselves and
> be their own judges obey the laws. Others sense their own laws
> within them; things are forbidden to them that every honorable
> man will do any day in the year and other things are allowed
> to them that are generally despised. Each person must stand
> on his own feet.
>
> > Max Demian speaking to Sinclair in
> > Hermann Hesse's novel, *Demian*

TURNER: These passages should make you a bit uncomfortable. Nietzsche and his novelist disciple, Hesse, propound an extreme view of "do-it-yourself morality," according to which man can and must create his own values. You seem to be rushing headlong in that same general direction, by your concentration on an individual's private efforts to "transcend alienation" or "subjugate his temperamental inclination" as the source of moral good. But I don't mean to single you out. There are others who are equally subjectivist[1] in their orientation – Descartes, Rousseau, Kant, Kierkegaard. In the "old days," it used to be the case that the idea of God, often conjoined with an authoritarian church and/or state, gave teeth and clout to the "moral law."

But with the advent of "Enlightenment" and new-fangled democratic trends, the philosophers I've just mentioned (and others as well) deemed it necessary to take the place of God and the church and/or state, and bolster up the sagging cause of morality by appealing to the power of human consciousness, whether to establish the existence of God as supreme moralist or to directly impose dire and absolute duties upon the human race. Nietzsche finally brought all these currents to their logical terminus, by proposing that man could and should hoist and balance the heavens of morality upon his own shoulders, like a modern version of the Greek superman, Atlas. In our preceding discussion, you expressed the intimation that there must be some "common denominators," some objective referrents, which might form a nucleus for our consensus about morality in spite of our apparently highly divergent experiences of what morality is all about. I think this intimation is worth pursuing. But I wonder whether your very approach and presuppositions don't sentence you to failure at the outset. You are so locked into an excessively individualistic approach to morality that you have immunized yourself against objectivity in any form.

CRANSTON: Objectivity in *any* form? I would say that the only form of objectivity I'm "immunized" against is that objectivity that fails to give due deference to the individual, and the sort of creative individual moral insights that Nietzsche and others have taken such pains to defend. I'm not so sure that individual insights are the antitheses of objectivity, as you seem to think. It may just be the case that the proper womb for the gestation and delivery of "objectivity" in the paramount sense of the word, is the often maligned consciousness of the private individual. Would you look elsewhere for objectivity?

TURNER: I think I am in favor of "the individual" as much as you are. However, I am opposed to portraying as "private" what is public in the life and experience of individuals. And there is an aspect of morality that is *preeminently* public. That is the "objective" morality you are asking about.

I think I have already made it quite clear in our discussion of the "HM-ought" that I believe there are certain modes of behavior which are more conducive to happiness than others. Insofar as individuals are not completely different or hidden from our purview, it is possible to find some common convergences, generalize on these, and apply them through socio-cultural channels to most people. This generalization and institutionalization of privileged practices is "objective" morality.

CRANSTON: A morality would not be *truly* objective unless it corresponded to some basic aspirations and needs of man (and not just men in this or that socio-cultural situation). I have no objections to your attempt to generalize about human behavior; but you're not going far enough, not digging deep enough, not setting your standards high enough. An "objective" morality should be applicable to all men living at all times, for "everyman."

TURNER: I'm beginning to see why you tend towards a *de facto* subjectivistic position: you set your standards for objectivity so high that they are well nigh humanly unattainable. Let's take a closer look at your assertion: It makes a *big* difference whether we are talking about a *general* action or a specific and *particular* action being "right" or "wrong" for "all people at all times." I wouldn't want to have the job of justifying the statement that "homicide is wrong for all people at all times." However, I would feel differently about the statement "killing your best friend who has done nothing wrong to you, simply for the motive of drinking the blood in his veins (which you happen to prefer to Martinis), is wrong for all people at all times." I could go along with that. Would you like to make an absolute Kantian categorical imperative[2] out of that?

CRANSTON: You don't feel a definite and real sense of obligation and duty, in subscribing to that statement?

TURNER: No, I just feel my happiness and the happiness of others would definitely be infringed on, if people were to do things like this.

CRANSTON: Would you go so far as to impose these feelings on others?

TURNER: I believe that sophisticated conditioning through positive reinforcement and a well-organized social system can prevent outbreaks of such behavior. But if, in certain cases, that is not enough, and if I were in the position to decide what was to be done, I would wack offenders with the appropriate punishment, to put them out of commission and warn other potential offenders.

CRANSTON: Nietzsche also speculates that, if and when any of his moral Supermen get into a position of political power, they should impose their morality on the masses by a similar system of incentives and deterrents.

TURNER: All right. But there's a big difference between my pragmatic policies and Nietzsche's prescription for living. I am for inculcating certain rules of behavior which are generally accepted as conducive to human welfare or happiness, while our friend Nietzsche wants to impose some mysterious creative urging that he feels in the deepest recesses of his transformed psyche. This latter brand of imposition is another subtle variation in that long tradition of moral mystification that we were speaking about, and I think you will agree, could even be quite dangerous to humanity in these days of laser beams and nuclear warheads.

CRANSTON: When you get down to the nitty gritty of it all, I wonder whether it is any more dangerous to be ruled by a semi-mystical and ascetic

Nietzschean Superman than by a self-styled interpreter and defender of the "public happiness."

TURNER: That is a choice you will have to make in the sacred privacy of your own conscience. I do hope you make your decision in favor of us "good guys" ...

CRANSTON: What if you run into others who have sharply divergent views about happiness, or even oppose sharply divergent notions of duty to your ideas of happiness? Don't you feel some need to *justify* your view? And if you try to justify it, aren't you really, in essence, trying to show (in an intellectual way, and without simply pointing to a *fait accompli* in the public domain) that it is more "objective" than the opposing views?

TURNER: If my view was definitely the majority view, I would not have much need to justify it. It would be the prevailing view. If I were in the minority, I might make some efforts to show the majority how my view might be more conducive to their happiness. However, if I couldn't do that, I would have to sit back and keep quiet, because the majority has the "last word" regarding objectivity, even in the face of my able intellectualizations. I'm afraid this is an unsatisfactory answer for you. But what else am I to say? That I have some basic intuition or even proof of what is objectively right, and every other normal person should have the same intuition? I can't go that route.

CRANSTON: And you feel "the majority" may be able to produce an objective morality if you just sit back and let them do their "thing"?

TURNER: Certainly not "objective" in the sense of something prevailing for all times and places and people. But "objective" in the sense of a prevailing public morality. That's objective enough for me. If I happen to disagree with the prevailing morality, then – let's face it – *my* morality is not going to be "objective."

CRANSTON: And yet, while admitting that that prevailing morality is "objective," you would still argue with the majority that the standards you yourself support ought to prevail? That doesn't sound self-consistent to me.

TURNER: In arguing in this vein I would simply be trying to persuade them that my view would be more satisfying *if* it became objective. We obviously have different views about what "objective" means.

CRANSTON: Yes. You're simply talking about what would be the "objective" morality for this or that particular society. I would call that "relativistic" morality rather than objective morality.

TURNER: Why not call it an "absolutism" – since I am saying that whatever objective morality there is, must be "absolutely" determined by the needs and choices of a particular society.

CRANSTON: You know this is not the way "objective" and "relative" are usually used. We've got to adhere to common meanings if we're going to have any progress in communication.

TURNER: But these thoughts seem to be "dialectical" considerations, and I thought that you, if anyone, would appreciate them ... At any rate, I've said these things to show that I am not a "subjectivist" simply because I cannot identify with the extraordinarily high standards for objectivity *you* would like to set.

CRANSTON: I'm not so sure you've managed to maintain health and equilibrium by your resolute refusal to go to subjective "extremes." There seems to be a kind of schizophrenic split between what you previously called the HM-ought and what you now refer to as "objective" morality. In this present discussion[3] you tried briefly to portray the latter as a kind of generalization from the former. But I certainly don't see the logic of the leap from the one to the other, and I suspect that they are antithetical rather than consanguineous concepts.

TURNER: You're quite right. There is no "necessary" relationship between the public or "objective" morality and the HM-oughts of individuals. The "public morality" gives a sort of summary expression to all these HM-oughts, and I would certainly hope that many of my own HM-oughts are so expressed. But whether they are or not is a contingency.

CRANSTON: A matter of luck?

TURNER: A matter of numbers, fashions, pressures, needs of the time, and so forth.

CRANSTON: You wouldn't go so far as to say that any of your especially valued HM-oughts "ought" to be incorporated into the public morality?

TURNER: If I said that, I would simply *mean* that I hoped as many as posssible of my conceptions of happiness became incorporated or reflected in the prevailing public morality. But you, of course, would prefer a stronger statement?

CRANSTON: I would. I find it odious and arbitrary to resign myself to the purely arbitrary relationship between individual aspirations and public standards which you seem to be satisfied with. It seems to me there must be some kind of "middle-ground" between Nietzschean subjectivism and the sort of resignation to the norms-that-be, that you recommend. I'm thinking of something like the Kantian Categorical Imperative. Kant's idea that a moral norm would be "objective" if one could mentally universalize it for all men, including himself, avoided the extremely private characteristics of Nietzschean morality, but still fell short of appealing to actual social or public practices for confirmation. It was the natural "middle-ground."

TURNER: But, as you know, the universalization hypothesis has had a rough time ever since it's birth in minds like Kant's. Not only rogues like Hegel, but suave and sophisticated practitioners of philosophy in more recent times have demonstrated the difficulty of actually applying this hypothesis to instances of human behavior.

I have to admit that when I am reading Kant, and I follow the examples and applications he offers for his "categorical imperative,"[4] I get the transitory feeling that he is really offering a valid means for testing the "objectivity" of moral norms. But then when I follow through on his or my own concrete applications, it seems impossible to maintain consistency. Take, for example, the moral norms on homicide which we were discussing. On the one hand, when you apply the universalizability criterion and ask yourself, "would I want homicide to become the universal norm of behavior for everyone else as well as myself," the intuitive response comes loud and clear as a resounding "no"! But when we try to get just a little more specific, and adjudicate whether e.g. homicide is permissable in a defensive war, or in the punishment of dangerous and unrepentant criminals, the universalizability criterion no longer looks very helpful. If I happen to fear that society, even without good reason, may at sometime in the future put *me* in the category of "dangerous and unrepentant criminal," I am going to formulate *my* categorical imperative this way: "Would I want capital punishment to be meted out at all times and in all places *even by a fickle and unfair* society to such-and-such criminals"? If I happen to be a conscientious objector, I will formulate *my* categorical imperative about war in this way: "Would I want homicide to be a rule of behavior in defensive wars, *even for combatants who have religious or moral qualms about any form of killing"?* And so forth. In other words, if I have a subjective interest in the outcome, I can always formulate the categorical imperative in such a way that it favors and promotes my interests.

CRANSTON: And that, of course, is why Kant insists on formulating his categorical imperatives in such a way that it will expressly preclude all the "ifs," i.e. the exceptions and extenuating factors.

TURNER: Which is absurd. Because what he would like to call an "exception" is very often an important and relevant factor which should be taken into consideration in making a moral judgement.

CRANSTON: One has to draw some limits as to the factors which are to be considered relevant to the making of this or that moral judgement. Otherwise, we must be resigned to bringing in the sum-total of individuating factors which precisely distinguish each person from others – and in consequence we would be trying to tailor-make an individual morality to suit each person. I'm sure you wouldn't want to go to that extreme.

TURNER: No. You're quite right. There *are* limits as to the factors which should be considered relevant to the making of moral judgements. But these are the limited number of consequences that individuals, making use of all the informational means and consultations available to them, can reasonably discern as probably resulting from a contemplated action. As one who does not have divine foresight or prophetic powers applies such pragmatic[5] or utilitarian[6] criteria, he certainly places himself under definite limitations as to the number of variables he will consider; but he at least has an advantage over the Kantian in appealing to publicly observable and reasonably objective factors in coming up with his own objective judgement.

CRANSTON: I'm not so sure about that. To use the examples you cited above, your "utilitarian" conscientious objector and potential accused-criminal will manage to focus on certain "objective" effects or consequences which happen to favor their own cause and make their decision on this basis. The potential accused-criminal will talk about the "possible effects to society" if the judicial machinery does not meticulously avoid shortcuts and accelerations which might tend to threaten innocent persons (defined as people like himself) with incarceration; the conscientious objector of the utilitarian variety will speak about the ultimate possibility of citizens being needlessly killed if people (i.e. idealistic people like himself, who have judged war or a particular war "unjust") are forced to fight a nation's wars. Perhaps the only way out of such difficulties would be to preface all such considerations with a prior second-order[7] categorical imperative emphasizing altruism and social consciousness: for example, I would have to ask, "would I want any individual to consider his selfish interests paramount, in coming up with his application of the utilitarian formula"? If I answer "no" to this, then I would have to conclude in Kantian fashion that altruism should be a universal rule for everyone, and to be consistent, I would have to refrain from bringing in selfish considerations when I did my utilitarian "thing."

TURNER: The only problem is, the individual who prefaces his moral judgements with that second-order categorical imperative would tend (if he is *really* and blindly selfish) to define "unselfish" interests as his own interest, and selfish" interests as those of others. Also, I think you should realize that there is no way of formulating even that "second-order" categorical imperative without at least some reference to pragmatic criteria. When you're asking your question about the individual and his selfish "interests," you are really contemplating the *effects* that such emphasis on selfish interests would have on society as a whole.

CRANSTON: You're not going to tell me that *altruism* could best be boosted by a resort to pragmatic considerations?

TURNER: Not at all. It would turn out the other way. I'm sure that most people in *our* society, if they consider *all* the consequences, would end up on the side of their individual interest (call this "selfishness," if you will).

CRANSTON: Let us say that they did go through some such pragmatic process of adjudication, and come up on the side of "individual interests." Then in the next breath, being good utilitarians, they state that their goal is "the greatest good of the greatest number." I discern a contradiction here. If the individual's own private pursuit of happiness is the primal utilitarian objective, why not state the objective in those terms? Anyone who hears the utilitarian formula would take it as a thrust towards altruism. But it's really covert egoism, if I understand you correctly.

TURNER: Not necessarily so. The "greatest happiness of the greatest number" is in a way a means for facilitating the *individual* pursuit of happiness. When a sufficient number of individuals are engaged in pursuing their own personal happiness, they find, often unfortunately by trial and error, that they have to raise their sights to encompass the happiness of the majority, just to secure and foster their own happiness. Now if you went and asked each individual whether he was seeking the communal happiness as an end-in-itself or as a means to some further good, most would probably answer honestly that it was sought as a means to personal fulfillment, if they reflected on the matter and their own motives sufficiently. But don't be taken aback at this.

CRANSTON: I won't. I suspect that a Kantian egoist would find a way to universalize egoism (*his* favorite "objective" moral norm) while the Kantian altruist would end up emphasizing altruism (the moral norm that truly applied to everybody). However, I react instinctively against your unabashed defense of egoism. I wouldn't want to say that the individual's happiness has to be *subordinated* to that of the majority, but it seems intuitively clear to me that a kind of equilibrium between egoism and altruism should be maintained; or, in other words, that one shouldn't desire things for himself that he wouldn't want others of equal worth and capacities and in equal situations to also enjoy.

TURNER: I think that is an admirable, if somewhat idealistic way of looking at things. In any case, it is something you hold on a purely intuitive basis. Now, I think I would agree with your essential intuition: that there should be a kind of fundamental "equilibrium" between egoism and altruism; that neither one should get the better of the other, so to speak. But this is no "objective" principle. It's just two people who happen to have the same intuition; and if the public morality dictates something other than this equilibrium as a norm, we can't use a categorical imperative or any other instrument that I'm familiar with to mold or pound it into something beyond a mere intuition,[8] i.e. into an objective moral principle. Instead of beginning with ideals and intuitions, why don't you focus on the "public morality"? I think we have a better chance of arriving at an understanding of objectivity *via* that route.

CRANSTON: I have no objection against concentrating on the "public morality," but I am looking for something a little different there than you are. I would like to focus on those moral laws present now which happen to have something perennial about them. As a matter of fact, these perennial norms hold promise of being the sort of "middle term" I am looking for. For if we can find certain prevailing norms which have prevailed for *all* cultures at all times, we will be able to avoid both the sort of Nietzschean subjectivism which you dislike and the sort of resignation to "the public morality" that I find objectionable, Yes, morality must *begin* with the individual and in consciousness. But it doesn't have to end there. It is quite possible, and, it seems to me, probable that some of the dictates of the conscience of the moral individual correspond to some laws governing the human race as a whole – in other words, that there is something in human nature itself corresponding to, and giving rise to, our moral insights. And a corollary: if one wants to test his moral insights for validity, the criterion to which he should turn is not the prevailing mores, but as much knowledge-in-depth as he can muster about human nature, with its special characteristics and exigencies.

TURNER: In other words, you're continuing the age-old search for a "natural law." I suspected earlier that you were going to end up in a "natural law" position,[9] but you managed to circumvent that necessity until now. But now you've made the leap. And it's a leap that's quite logical for you. You want to establish a general moral norm that is somehow *imposed* on human nature, and yet you don't want to say either *a)* that this norm is imposed by God as a command to be believed and followed without reasoning why, or *b)* that the norm is a remnant of an old Oedipus complex or early childhood fixations or repressions, or *c)* that it is simply akin to positive law and the prevailing customs which are "imposed" on us by past generations, prevailing social pressures, and the present regime. Your problem is finding a suitably severe "imposer" to give "clout" and real binding force to your "ought." And a natural candidate for that is "human nature" itself, which we can take to be a kind of hard taskmaster which imposes its laws on us willy-nilly, and at least in some cases imposes the same laws in all of us without exception. Don't you think it's a bit incongruous that you should object to my apparent abandonment to presently prevailing human standards, while you yourself would shamelessly like to abandon yourself to eternal or at least perennial human practices?

CRANSTON: No, a "natural law" would not be something that everyone does, but that everyone *should* do. I'll try to put in into your terms: A natural law would have to be a norm for behavior concerning which there has been a consensus in every society from time immemorial, such that every society was willing to command or prohibit such behavior, and back up their commands or prohibitions with sanctions or pressures of some sort. The fact that there are departures is not to the point, provided that such departures are consistently recognized as delinquencies.

TURNER: I might be able to go along with that formulation. But what's the purpose of this little exercise? Do you really think there is some such species of behavior?

CRANSTON: I think the prohibition against homicide might be the clearest example. There is a universal opprobrium attached to homicide throughout the civilized world, and anthropologists agree that it is prohibited in almost every culture. It is one of a very few taboos about which there is such universal agreement. If a moral norm applied to just about everyone living at any time, it would be a pretty close approximation to an "objective" norm, and even to a "natural law." Would you agree that the example of homicide I gave "fits the bill"?

TURNER: You've got a bad start in this reasoning process, because the facts you're beginning with are wrong, or at least distorted. The prohibition against homicide has always been a provincial prohibition. It has never seriously been extended to "all men," but only to one's tribe, or society, or nation, or kindred tribes or societies. Outside the stipulated boundaries the prohibition is relaxed. Even in our own "civilized" era, much the same situation prevails. The My Lai massacre of innocent villagers by American soldiers in Vietnam is considered by us to be *toto caelo* different than a sniper attack on innocent fellow-citizens by someone shooting from a tower in Texas.

CRANSTON: Very well. We could specify the prohibited brand of homicide more precisely as the killing in cold blood of someone who belongs to the in-group or in-groups recognized and protected by a particular culture or society.

TURNER: I would go along with that definition, but it would seem to destroy your argument. How could you say that the prohibition of homicide in particular circumstances or with regard to particular classes of people is a "universal law"? By the very use of the adjective, "particular," you're saying in effect that the law is *not* universal.

CRANSTON: Unless I define "homicide" precisely in terms of these particulars. Which is what I am doing. I am saying that such-and-such particulars (constituting the *definition* of homicide) are universally prohibited.

TURNER: If you could establish some kind of uniformity in the way that *everyone* defines these particulars, your definition might be representative and viable. But – let's say that you did do this satisfactorily. You would still be defeating your own present purpose. Take the example of homicide: If you succeed in showing that there is a universal prohibition of homicide *only with respect to one's own countrymen or race or kinsfolk*, I suppose one might reasonably deduce that there was something basically "unnatural" about flouting this prohibition. But the prohibition itself would still be a far cry from a "natural law" – at least if I have understood what you were trying to get at with that concept. For you and others who hearken to a "natural law" would like to use the natural law as a handle for intellectually separating yourself from your provincial environment, with its culture and mores, in order to pass value judgements on this environment from an absolutely impartial and objective and perhaps even eternal vantage point. You don't want "provincial" natural laws. You want laws which are not only universally extant but universally *applicable*. In regard to homicide you want a law which will throw light precisely on the more difficult cases, the cases where homicide has been committed against some out-group or some individual belonging to an out-group. A society has no great problem adjudicating cases of homicide affecting what is definitely recognized as an "in-group" in *that particular society*. The provincial natural law you have come up with would be "old hat" to that society: they would yawn after hearing your important principle, and simply answer "of course."

CRANSTON: I can see your point. But I would suggest that there is at least one candidate for the title of "natural law" which is *not* provincial in either prevalence or applicability. I am thinking of the "Golden Rule" – "do unto others as you would have them do unto you." There has been an extraordinary consensus about this rule in the major and minor cultures and religions of the world. This consensus is very often unrelated to any cross-cultural intellectual fertilization or even indirect influence. This, if anything, would be a "natural law." And the objection that it is provincial and esoteric would not seem to apply, in the way that it would apply with regard to murder. For the very concept of the "others" referred to in the Golden Rule comprises what we have called the "out group." The whole idea of the Golden Rule is that you should put *others* on an equal footing with yourself and those you identify with.

TURNER: I would say that your interpretation is in accord with the Christian version of the Golden Rule as expounded in the Sermon on the Mount in Matthew's Gospel,[10] where there are explicit recommendations of love for enemies and outsiders. But many of the non-Christian versions fall short of such universality and altruism.

CRANSTON: Is it really necessary to spell out as Christianity does, to what extent the "others" are "other"? The very word implies a reference to those who are different, strangers, etc.

TURNER: Depending on usage, "others" can be taken to mean *our* "others" (our alter-egos, those whom we consider to be separate but equal), or *the* "others" (those we don't like, don't understand, don't identify with). Yes, I think it's necessary to spell out the extension of the word. Since this is often not made clear, the universality which is concomitant to the Christian version cannot be taken to extend to all those other versions. So the Christian-type Golden Rule falls short of natural-law universality just as did the prohibition of homicide – but for different reasons. In the case of homicide, there was universality in prevalence, but not in its applicability; in the present instance, there is universality in applicability (i.e. even to enemies, etc.) but the incidence or prevalence of the rule *in that (Christian) form* appears to fall short of universality.

But let's say that it *did* turn out to be not only universally applicable but universally prevalent. What would this *prove?* We know for a fact that a hell of a lot of people in history have not followed *any* Golden Rule, and no society has ever enforced it, even if it were "on the books" in some local law enforcement agency's manual of rules or on the walls of some theologian's study.

CRANSTON: How could it be enforced on a people except by some very subtle moral pressures? I suspect that it has been enforced *that* way, and is still being enforced in that same way ... You ask me: what would it "prove" if the Golden Rule were universal in every important respect? It would prove that there was something in the psyche of other men in other cultures and civilizations which coincides in essential respects with sentiments and allegiances in our own psyche. I could quote poets like Horace and Goethe to show what I mean. But, of course, this wouldn"t amount to a rigorous scientific proof. Do you really need that sort of proof for something like this?

TURNER: For concluding that something like a universal Golden Rule might be related to certain sentiments or aspirations common to human beings? No, I could accept that on an intuitive basis, as long as we don't have to speak of "all" human beings. And, in fact, I would agree that these sentiments are quite meaningful. But I would interpret their meaning differently. You would like to see them as signposts all pointing unmistakably in the direction of a human "nature" as the cause and common source of such similar aspirations. I, for my part, see them as future-oriented. When you and others *say* that you have this deep common aspiration in favor of certain laws, such as the Golden Rule, what you mean is that you have such a satisfying conviction of the importance of such laws that you would like to see them extended (as soon as possible, but at some indefinite time in the future) to all men, so that they all can share in your satisfaction and corroborate your conviction. Now, I personally feel that that is a noble wish. But it's just a wish.

CRANSTON: The past is prologue for the future. A wish for the future wouldn't make sense, unless there were already a firm basis for it in human nature. But one doesn't have to wait for the wish to materialize before it can be considered objective and (if the wish is a moral one) morally objective.

Consider, for instance, the wish for the abolition of slavery. In times past slavery was almost universally accepted with moral approval, or at least with little moral repugnance. St. Paul the Apostle even wrote an epistle – *Philemon* – to a Christian slave-master asking him to accept back a newly converted runaway slave, without punishing him too severely. Do you think the fact that slavery was so widely accepted as a feature of the "public morality" at the time is sufficient justification for calling it an "objectively moral" practice? Wouldn't it make more sense to say that there was something objectively good and moral and natural or basically human about the wish for emancipation itself, *even* in the days of slavery, that caused the wish to eventually "*catch on*" and become successful. Does the wish become valid and objective because people accept it, or do people accept it because it is valid and objectively best?

TURNER: In order to answer fully, I'd have to show how some ignoble and quite immoral wishes *also* caught on and became part of our public morality. But I could only show this to your satisfaction if you happened to be part of the small minority which did *not* subscribe to the public morality. Perhaps you would be willing to provide me with a list of actions currently considered "moral" by just about everybody, which you consider immoral: No? I don't blame you. Never give ammunition to the enemy ... But at any rate I think I can prove that the example you gave, of emancipation from slavery, does not really show what you think it does. You want to say that slavery was always immoral, even "way back when," and that the objective morality of emancipation, which had always been there as a seminal idea and a natural human imperative, simply required a more advanced state of moral consciousness before it "caught on." But I say that slavery was probably quite moral, quite objectively moral, in the days of St. Paul and Aristotle and other serious thinkers who accepted the practice. Taking into account the different economic structures in the ancient world, and the almost complete absence of any concept of freedom or independence in *our* sense among the masses at that time, it is quite probable that the practice of slavery was widely considered (by the masses as well as the elite) as contributing to "the greatest happiness of the greatest number." I might go even further and ask, are you sure that slavery has been eradicated now? Karl Marx says that "capitalistic relations' constitute the greatest, albeit the most subtle, form of slavery in the history of the world. Advocates of women's liberation now say that the domestication and subordination of women has been the most monumental accomplishment of slavery, and is only beginning to be realized and reversed. So I'm not so sure about all this "moral progress" that you seem to think is the result of certain moral ideas which are more valid and "objective" than others.

CRANSTON: To answer you comprehensively, I would have to be able to produce a thorough analysis of the history of an idea like slavery, through-out all of its major vicissitudes and applications. I'm not up to a task like that. But let me reduce my thesis to its bare bones: There is such a thing as an "idea whose time has come." In morality, we can't say this about just any idea, but only an idea that has unusual validity and yes, objectivity. Can you accept that much of the previous "package"?

TURNER: I see that the "natural law" position has undergone some subtle and interesting transformations under your direction. As you understand the meaning of a moral idea whose "time had come," this would connote an intrinsically valid idea that would inevitably "surface" and be recognized as objectively valid, but required the proper stage of human progress to be reached before this could take place. This is a thesis which essentially pre-supposes an upward and specifically moral *evolution* of the human race. Because you experienced such difficulty in maintaining that there is some basic law governing human nature at all times, you now come up with your "modified" position: that evolutionary progress, which includes moral pro-gress, *now* dictates such and-such a moral imperative, which now becomes tantamount to a "natural law" for all evolving individuals. Now, that's a nice thesis, but I have to tell you frankly: it doesn't have a chance of "getting off the ground" unless you can also show 1) that evolution is actually pro-gressive at all, and is still progressing forward or upward, rather than sliding back and deteriorating; and 2) that there is anything specifically moral about the evolutionary progress that takes place, and how we can satisfactorily differentiate the moral from the amoral or immoral types of progress. Can you show this?

CRANSTON: No, but neither do I consider myself bound to offer any apologetic for some contemporary evolutionary conception of "natural law." I had no intention of getting into such absolutely cosmic considerations when I made my remark about ideas whose "time had come." Let me try to put this into language which I think you may find more acceptable: Some moral ideas (or "wishes," if you like) have more important external and *social* bearings and ramifications than others. The fact that these ideas "catch on" is undoubtedly due in part to the external conditions which prepare the way for them, but partly also to the intrinsic "staying power" and validity of the ideas themselves. One might say that they are more "potentially" objective than many of their counterparts.

TURNER: Some of the pet ideals of Nietzsche's Superman[11] were "socially" oriented, too – towards imposing a "master" morality upon the unthinking masses. Would you say that those ideas have great "potential objectivity"?

CRANSTON: If one has to impose an idea by force, it shows he has little confidence in the intrinsic objectivity of that idea. The more force he feels it is necessary to use, the less faith he proclaims in his idea or ideal.

TURNER: As you said earlier, Nietzsche hypothesized that a superior morality could be imposed by a truly sophisticated Superman-statesman by the use of judicious persuasion and example, with little or no need of force from "on high. . . ."

CRANSTON: I would like to completely eschew the idea of arbitrary imposition in any of its pejorative senses, i.e. as comprising violence, thought-control, hypnotic suggestion, or propaganda. But if an idea "imposes" *itself* on human beings by its intrinsic attractiveness, that's a different matter. Isn't that the whole idea behind moral "*goodness*." People desire it because it is good, attractive, desirable.

TURNER: I believe you have considerably watered down the "oughts" and "obligations" you were referring to in some of our previous conversations. In fact, I almost feel attracted to *this* version of the "ought," myself. However, in your enthusiasm for championing the intrinsic attractiveness or desirability of moral ideals, you seem to be supposing that people desire them because they are desirable, whereas previously you held that they become desirable ("oughts") because people experience a supra-temperamental attraction for them. Which is the position that you want to identify with?

CRANSTON: Why do I have to choose? I would like to emphasize the fact that both of these aspects, which I would call the "subjective" and "objective" aspects, are equally important, and, in fact, inseparable reciprocals. It is only certain types of (subjective) desire which give rise to bona fide (objective) "oughts." It is only a certain species of (objective) "ought" which is desirable enough to elicit sustained and universal (subjective) approval in the social sphere.

TURNER: I don't think you can get off that easily. Subjective wills give rise to all sorts of superfluous and nonsensical oughts which plague us and our children. And moral ideas, no matter how intrinsically desirable, don't just present *themselves* for approval. They are presented by *people* with whims and prejudices and conscious or unconscious desires to see everyone else celebrating their pet idea or ideal. Your idea of a synthesis sounds very nice on paper, but, if realism is your concern, "it won't wash."

CRANSTON: Aristotle didn't seem to think that such a synthesis was unrealistic. You may recall a very brief passage in Aristotle's *Nichomachean Ethics*[12] where he is asking, what is the ultimate criterion for morality in any society? And he comes up with the solution: it is the exemplary individual, the man who by his very example epitomizes virtue and excellence for his society. Such a man is both the creator of morality (in the Nietzschean sense), and the objective criterion for morality; his desires give rise to the really significant "oughts," and the ideals which he exemplifies supply the objective criteria for morality in his milieu; the criteria become desirable because they are fostered by his exemplary desires, but he and others desire these criteria only because they are so intrinsically desirable in the first place.

TURNER: So now you have found the objectivity you were looking for: An *objective* exemplary *individual* who sets the standards and who manages to set such intrinsically objective standards that they are not just his private property but emerge almost "on their own steam" into the public domain. A truly Hegelian synthesis, with just a touch of paradox. I knew you could pull it off!

But you should really take a second look at this synthesis. It reminds me a bit of the problems that emerged when Plato came up with his own synthesis of a "philosopher king" in the *Republic*.[13] It was a nice idea to have a king who was also as wise as possible, i.e. a philosopher. But the whole training and orientation of the philosopher (as Plato depicted him) was to flee from public power and external recognition; while the impulses of kings and leaders flowed in the direction precisely opposite to that of the philosopher. So the resultant "synthesis" which offered a solution to some of the problems Plato raised in the *Republic*, turned out to be such a rare (i.e. nonexistent) bird that it was a "solution" only in name. Your synthesis has similar defects. An exemplary individual who would truly be an exemplar for his people, would have to be in a position of leadership or influence to function *as* an exemplar. However, those in this position, no matter how benevolent, are practising an imposition of sorts. It would be practically impossible for *them* to merely express or embody ideals which could "catch on" because of their *intrinsic* attractiveness. On the other hand, we can envision a host of truly incomparable individuals in hidden corners of the world who embody a higher and, to use your terminology, a potentially more objective but actually subjective morality than the value-makers. But the fact that they have attained such a high degree of subjective morality is no doubt due in great part to the fact that they *haven't* been busying themselves with imposing their values on others. So the idea of the "exemplary virtuous individual" seems to be as mythical as Plato's "philosopher king." If one pursues intrinsic good and morality, he can't operate efficiently and "full-time" in an extrinsic function as an exemplar-for-others. If he influences others and even unconsciously imposes his values on them, we can never be sure that the reactions to his values are based on their intrinsic desirability.

CRANSTON: I'm not willing to admit that the exemplary individual cannot exist at all. Sometimes I think I am a bit more optimistic about men and the state of humanity than you.

TURNER: Surely, your exemplary individual might exist, but only in a quasi-Platonic meritocracy in which virtue was synonymous with power, and the only power that was wielded was the power of ideas and example. Only amid such structures could our archetypal but anomalous individual exercise power in the very act of cultivating virtue, and suffer scarcely any temptation to depart from "the path of virtue" to control or pressure others by amoral or immoral means. As you can see, it is only a sterile utopian ideal that can supply a suitable cradle for the birth of your exemplary individual.

CRANSTON: You do admit, however, that if suitable conditions obtained, the "exemplary individual" would offer us a kind of "middle-term" objectivity.

TURNER: I think I can grant you that.

CRANSTON: You may have to make a similar concession to Nietzsche. You may recall his "Zarathustra" in one place hears approvingly the aspirations of two kings to the effect that the truly superior individual will one day actually wield power in this world.[14] So you are wrong at least in your imputation of an extremely "subjectivist" view of morality to Nietzsche. He opted for quite an objective criterion – a single individual who would incorporate and exemplify the effective standards of morality for his fellows.

TURNER: Very well. I hadn't thought of Nietzsche in connection with this rather esoteric brand of "objectivity." But at any rate, Nietzsche's synthesis begins to disintegrate upon inspection just as does Plato's (and your own, too, I'm afraid) – and for the reasons I've just adumbrated.

CRANSTON: Then not even the most extraordinary individual paragon of virtue could boast, for you, a truly "objective" brand of morality, if he contradicted the standards of the public morality. The "public morality" is objectively moral, for you, even if it's immoral. It's that simple.

TURNER: Don't get me wrong. I sincerely sympathize with your intuition that there are some moral aspirations which seem to be "potentially" more objective than others. But I would like to warn you, don't treat this "potential" objectivity as a kind of second-best but nevertheless real objectivity. I would like to reiterate: it's no objectivity at all unless it becomes actually incorporated into the public realm. I think I can demonstrate this by an analogy from aesthetics: You might say there's something "objectively aesthetic" about the work of the poet who writes extraordinary poems that no one ever reads, or the painter who produces fantastic paintings that no one ever sees. You might say that both of them are producing potentially great works of art. But let's face it, what they produce cannot be truly "great" works of art (in the usual sense of that adjective) or objective epitomes of artistic expression until they are accepted, and widely accepted. In line with this analogy, the morality of the exemplary individuals has to become reflected in the public realm or embodied in laws, customs and institutions, before it becomes *truly* "objective." In a world where no system of "natural law" is operative or at least recognized, the objectivity of morality consists in its embodiment in the sort of "public" accountrements that I have mentioned.

CRANSTON: It's becoming clear to me that you are confusing two different meanings of "objectivity." "Objective" sometimes means "external and observable" (as opposed to "subjectivity" as something hidden within the psyche) but at other times means a standard or indisputable criterion (as opposed to "subjectivity" as something capricious and individualistic). It goes without saying that whatever morality there is may become "objective" in the first sense (objectivity$_1$) in the socio-political world. But it seems just too convenient that *this* "public morality" should also happen to offer the standard of "objective" morality in the second sense (objectivity$_2$).

Kant's categorical imperative has proved deficient for just the converse reason: it was clearly objective$_2$ in providing a universal standard, but shunned objectivity$_1$ since it expressly prescinded from any concrete, factual conditions or practices.

"Natural law" would have offered us a better possibility for uniting the two senses of objectivity, if only we had been able to produce an unequivocal example of a moral law which was both universally extant and universally applicable.

The "exemplary individual," on the other hand does effectively unite these two senses of objectivity, but only for an ideal society.

TURNER: I think that is a fair summary of where we have come in this discussion. But of course I don't agree with you that the dual (or "synthetic") function of the public morality in uniting both senses of objectivity is "too convenient" to be true. It's simply a fact of life that this is "objectivity" in the paramount sense. I'll try to establish this more to your satisfaction in our next encounter.

CHAPTER V

ETHICS AND POLITICS

If there is some *end* of the things we do, which we desire for
its own sake, ... clearly this must be the good and the chief
good. Will not the knowledge of it, then, have a great influence
on life? Shall we not, like archers who have a mark to aim at,
be more likely to hit upon what is right? If so, we must try, in
outline at least, to determine what [this end, which is the chief
good] is, and of which of the sciences or capacities it is the
object. It would seem to belong to the most authoritative art
and that which is most truly the master art. And politics appears
to be of this nature ... Our inquiry [into ethics] ... is political science, in one sense of the term.

Aristotle,[1] *Nichomachean Ethics*, I, 2

The political state is the actuality of the ethical idea. In the
state the concrete will (which thinks and knows and accom-
plishes what it knows just to the extent *that* it knows it) becomes fully revealed as the ethical spirit.

Hegel,[2] *The Philosophy of Right*, § 257

TURNER: In some of our previous conversations, you seem to have been
scandalized at the emphasis I placed on the "public morality" as the ultimate objective criterion for morality in general. Perhaps the passages I
have just cited may help you to see my position in its proper perspective. It
so happens that there are certain aspects of morality – let us call these the
"objective" aspects – which converge with what we call "socio-political"
considerations, and at a certain point become indistinguishable from the
latter. You don't seem to recognize this.

CRANSTON: You misconstrue both of those passages which you cite. It is
true that Aristotle stresses social ethics,[3] but he does not completely ignore
questions of individual responsibility and individual decision-making, and
the power and right of the individual to initiate changes in the socio-political
sphere. And as for Hegel, you may or may not be aware of the fact that he
makes a sharp distinction between "morality," which he sees as essentially
subjective, and "ethics," which he calls "objective spirit."

TURNER: That Hegelian terminology is confusing, since some contemporary ethicists say just the opposite: that "ethics" is subjective, while "morality"is objective. I suppose they may be doing this because of the etymological relationship of "morals" to "mores." At any rate, my point is that Hegel definitely considered the socio-political stages of morality or ethics to be more advanced and important than the subjective ones. And in Aristotle there is hardly any concentration on what we might call "individual" morality, but a systematic teleological subordination of private to public or social morality.

CRANSTON: To hear you citing Hegel for corroboration of your position is like listening to the Devil quoting scripture (excuse the comparison). You have often expressed opposition to Hegel's whole dialectical system. How can you use him in confirmation of your beliefs?

TURNER: I certainly have no sympathy whatsoever for his attempt to derive objective reality out of some "Absolute Idea"[4] – that's definitely "going off the deep end." But, to give credit where it is due, I consider his emphasis on the *ethical* import of the family, middle-class social relations, and governmental structures as a much-needed antidote during his own time to excessive Kantian subjectivism.[5] He, and Aristotle before him, seemed to have a healthy realization that, if you want to find objectivity$_2$ (to use the terminology you introduced in our last discussion), the first and most obvious place to look for it is objectivity$_1$. People derive their standards from the standards that happen to have become extant in their society. If their standards are minority standards, that is because they identify with a minority in their society and derive their standards from that minority. To contemplate individuals creating their moral norms *ex nihilo* or spider-like out of some inner substance of their consciousness is like trying to conceptualize a fetus growing on its own outside the womb. In more ways that we might like to admit, our values are formed by our society, or some segment of it, and its ways are our ways.

CRANSTON: And society is formed from the people in it. And these people often play a considerable role in determining *what* sort of things become objective$_{1 \& 2}$ in their society. You talk as if you are not concerned about what norms become "objective" in your society, as if it didn't matter.

TURNER: Of course it matters. People should do what they can to make sure that only the best sort of values surface in their society. But, try as they may, *they* cannot make a given set of values objective$_{1 \text{ or } 2}$. If a society as a whole says that eating cow flesh is wrong. I may disagree with that society but I cannot make my personal values objective in *any* sense.

CRANSTON: Please don't tell my children about this. I would like them to be optimistic about human life and progress.

TURNER: So you're afraid certain chaotic or egotistical or diabolical customs may implant their roots in the commonweal and develop into large and ugly and "immoral" but popularly acclaimed growths. Yes, that might happen. And then what you and I call "immoral" might become "objective $_{1\ \&\ 2}$ morality" for a few years. However, if it makes you feel any better, really chaotic or grossly egotistical ideas are not known to contribute in any outstanding way to national unity and stability. They don't have what you might call "staying power." But, of course, I can't guarantee that they will disappear overnight.

CRANSTON: I'm sure if you reflect on this matter a bit more intently, you would not be so liberal and permissive about the sort of external laws, customs and patterns of behavior which you would be willing to dub "objective$_{1\ \&\ 2}$ morality." Consider the following analogy between the individual and the state: We consider it to be important that every individual, no matter what he does, should be expressing himself, i.e. not some false or forced persona that he assumes ...

TURNER: I can't agree to that. I can think of some people whom I would wish would not express themselves at all. I would prefer that they repress their true personality or at least keep it pleasantly disguised.

CRANSTON: That's because *you* think there is something "false" about their true personality. You see, we're getting into semantical problems. Let's take a look at a couple of examples that we may be able to agree on: 1) Mental disease. A person suffering a neurosis or psychosis is "not himself" or "not herself." There seems to be something impeding the expression of self. That's why we call such people "mentally ill." And if they themselves seek treatment for mental illness, it means they have recognized that there's some lack of correspondence between the self that is "coming across," and the self that they really feel is there and should be coming across. 2) Criminality. I don't think either one of us would like to say that there is something *innately* evil about what we would call the "hardened criminal." We might consider an individual criminal unrepentant and unrehabilitable, but if we were asked how he *got* that way, we would point to causative factors such as bad heredity, bad upbringing or regrettable choices. In pointing out these factors, we are implicitly saying that, if it were not for such factors, the criminal would no doubt be able to express his true or better self, and would not have become a "criminal."

TURNER: Not everyone is as liberal as we are. Some would say that some "selves" are innately evil.

CRANSTON: Then I could not expect them to agree to the premises I am trying to establish here. But can *you* agree to them? Would you be willing to say that, at least in the sort of examples I've mentioned, there is a lack of correspondence between the inner self and its outer manifestations.

TURNER: I don't like this "inner-outer" terminology, which, of course, is designed to run parallel to that "ideal vs. empirical self" dichotomy that you brought up in a previous discussion. All I would want to say here is that these criminal types or the insane are not expressing the sort of self that *we* consider normal, so we come up with an appropriately descriptive designation ("insanity," "criminality") to let them, and everyone else, know that we disapprove of this sort of self- (or non-self-) expression.

CRANSTON: That's good enough for me. Now, the point I'm trying to make here is that, just as we disapprove of individuals who do not express what we would call a true self, so also we disapprove of socio-political structures which do not express the values and inner moral life of those who are living within these structures. Throughout most of our discussions, you have been emphasizing the fact that the structures and the controlling powers determine what is to be the "objective morality." I would now like to show you that the "other side of the coin" is equally important.

TURNER: That's a good point. But it all depends upon the *type* of socio-political structures in question. In a bona fide *democracy*, this would be the case. For a democracy, at least according to the classical definition,[6] is supposed to be a government whose policies, values and structures are determined by the people who constitute it. So what you are saying, if it applied at all, would seem to apply only to strictly democratic governments or reasonable facsimiles. But even if it did apply in the case of a democracy, this would not weaken the thrust of what I am saying one whit: A democratic government is one which encourages and constantly *conditions* its citizens to participate in controlling the structures, and to incorporate their personal values into the web and woof of these structures. So this appreciation of participation and incorporation is itself one of the "objective" values that citizens *in a democracy* derive from their polity.

CRANSTON: I'm afraid you've been engaging in academicism too long. You don't seem to realize that no governmental administration, even a democratic one, is going to encourage and even "condition" its citizens to stipulate and determine the official policies and moral values of the government.

TURNER: Then it wouldn't be democratic, at least in the classical sense.

CRANSTON: You may have something there. Is there *any* major democratic society existent now, in that classical sense? But still, I don't think the general thesis I'm developing here need necessarily be confined to democracy in any sense. It has a wider application. Have you heard of the Platonic-Aristotelian differentiation of governments on the basis of values predominating in their respective citizenries?

TURNER: Yes. Democracies are created and supported by citizens who value liberty, aristocracies by those who value excellence, oligarchies by those who desire wealth, etc. Montesquieu tried to come up with a similar axiological rule-of-thumb for classifying governments in the Rennaissance. None of this seems to have much relevance to present forms of government, anyway.

CRANSTON: Let me try to bring the classification up-to-date by suggesting the following extensions: a modern democracy reflects the predominating predilection of its citizens for individual rights and liberties; a nationalist government relies on and reflects national or ethnic pride; communist and socialist governments reflect a prevailing sentiment in favor of various degrees of equality. This isn't meant to be an absolutely exact classification, and of course other values will come into play besides the single "predominating" value that is mentioned in each case. But could you agree that the correspondence might stack up something like this.

TURNER: Yes. Maybe. I guess so. I warn you, I see exactly what you're leading up to, and it's not going to work. You want to try to show that the value system inculcated by any government is based, or *should be* based, on the "virtues" of its citizenry, rather than vice versa. That is something that could never be proven. And it becomes especially doubtful in non-democratic forms of government.

CRANSTON: The sort of "input" that takes place from the citizens is obviously different in a monarchy, or a socialist or nationalist society. But the fact that "non-democratic" governments do not have elections or referenda, or conduct their elections the way we do, does not necessarily mean there is a complete absence of such input.

TURNER: "Non-democratic governments" is a broad category. What about fascism and totalitarian communism. Do you think these governments are just expressions of the basic "virtues" of the people concerned?

CRANSTON: You already indicated the proper answer to your own question a minute ago, when you made a distinction between a governmental value system which "*is* based," and one which "*should* be based," on the virtues of its citizenry. Fascism, etc. obviously belong to the latter category. They are governments which should be based at least implicitly on the positive virtues of the people concerned, but they are not. In lieu of citizen input, they rely on propaganda, mind-control, torture and restriction of communication, transportation and ordinary congress. The citizens are "programmed" by the government rather than influencing the government in any direct or indirect way. And that, in a nutshell, is why such governments, at least, do not exemplify objective$_2$ morality.

TURNER: There's a saying that people by their provincialism or viciousness or apathy often end up getting the government they deserve ...

CRANSTON: That's cruel.

TURNER: Look, I'm willing to say that every government *should* in some way or other express the values and virtues of its citizenry, and even have systematic, organized procedures for facilitating this. But let's face it. I say that because I'm in a democratic milieu. And you proposed this criterion because you have lived in, and imbibed your values from the same milieu. But let's not make the mistake of saying that because what we call "democracy" is the "objective$_{1 \& 2}$ morality" for *us*, it should be for everyone else.

CRANSTON: Wait a minute. What's the degree of your commitment to democracy? Is it just because you happen to live under a democratic system that you believe governments should reflect the values of their citizens?

TURNER: In the last analysis, it probably is. And sometimes when I see the results of democratic procedures, I begin to have doubts about the universal preferability of democracy. Hitler was chosen as president and chancellor of Germany in a free plebiscite, and that was the end of democracy as well as sanity in that country.

CRANSTON: That was a sham plebiscite. As I've already indicated, the existence of propaganda, intimidation, etc. can render all "democratic" input shallow and meaningless.

TURNER: I'm not so sure that equivalent or greater pressures – although perhaps more subtle ones – might not be employed now or in the future in our own system, producing similar results, a sham democracy with sham elections.

CRANSTON: We're getting into the same sort of difficulty now that we encountered in our conversation on "is and ought," where the problem of ascertaining a "pure" natural impulse against homicide was brought up. I think there comes a time when we simply have to trust our intuition. In the present case, if we see the apparatus of democracy functioning, with freedom of the press and plenty of room for dissent and constructive criticism, we've got to overcome our scepticism and say "that's a government in which the values of the people are reflected and incorporated."

TURNER: Would you want this to be the case even if the people were vicious bums?

CRANSTON: But certainly – if the people were that enthusiastic and interested in their government, they wouldn't be "vicious bums," according to our definition.

TURNER: Do you really think that your "democratic criterion" – "the public morality of governments should reflect the values of their citizenry" –

could be used as a kind of subjective "test" for the "objectivity$_2$" of the morality of a particular government. Being aware of what happens to the Kantian test for morality when it is actually applied, you ought to be wary of introducing your own test for morality in government. It might boomerang on you.

CRANSTON: Our government would have greater reason to be wary of the test. I think it's obvious that, if this criterion were applied, certain prevalent governmental practices would be clearly demonstrated to be definitely deficient in objective$_2$ morality. For example, secrecy in government effectively denies its citizens the right to offer an educated and enlightened "input" to their government, since they don't know what's going on. Therefore secrecy must be jettisoned. And it is obvious that, if there *were* the requisite input, politicians in the executive branch would not easily be able to start wars that the citizens are going to have to fight and pay for. It is equally clear that so-called "intelligence activities" which border on atrocity and flout the moral standards of the citizens whose standards are supposed to be represented, would not be permitted.

TURNER: Should I take this as a scathing denunciation of our present democratic system?

CRANSTON: Not at all. The very fact that we are aware that things like this are going on, and that we are doing something about this awareness – shows we're on the right track.

TURNER: I hate to bring this up, but your advocacy of "input" by the "people" was just as ambiguous as it was noble and edifying. There are in our government various special interest groups and corporations which exert a lot of influence on the government sometimes through legal means such as lobbies and the financial support of various candidates for office, sometimes by illegal means such as bribery and payoffs (and there are also other means with all the shades of grey between the "legal" and "illegal" means). Would you include these under the umbrella term, "the people"? And would you call this influence "input"?

CRANSTON: This raises the problem of the proper balance of minority vs. majority rights, which is a delicate and difficult issue in political philosophy.

TURNER: Let's not get into that. There's really no need to, since, in spite of this little inquisition I have been conducting, I actually feel no great disagreement with you in regard to your basic thesis, that some sort of "real input" (however that could ever be defined) is necessary to assure the objective$_2$ validity of a government. But I am beginning to see now where our basic disagreement lies. First of all, to recapitulate: in my opinion the objectivity$_2$ of this "democratic thesis" is derived purely and simply from the objectivity$_{1\&2}$ of the public morality fostered by the particular socio-political structures in question. But to your mind this public morality is only an objectivity$_1$ and must derive its objectivity$_2$ from "the people" in some sense or other. Is that a fair statement?

CRANSTON: That's a rough outline of the two divergent directions in which we've been proceeding.

TURNER: O.K. Now there is a basic defect in your thesis. You want to say that the objectivity$_2$ of the objective$_1$ morality is derived from the values of the individual citizen (who constitutes the "inner" life of a nation). But you're unable to specify in any way which values of which citizens should prevail.

CRANSTON: We should use appropriately qualitative criteria to determine this: the degree of rational contribution and commitment to the values of their government on the part of the citizenry, the extent to which they make sure that the government is their own and keep themselves free from mere fashion and nostrums and the herding instinct.

TURNER: When you got down to the nitty-gritty of trying to make such determinations, I'm afraid you would find to your chagrin that quantitative measurements become necessary: In order to measure citizen contribution to government, we would have to isolate various contributions, rate them according to some scale, and compare citizens among themselves on this basis. In order to determine the degree of citizen commitment to govern-mental values we would have to utilize opinion polls and similar reckoning devices. In order to determine the extent of enlightened citizen participation in government, we would have to bring in quantitative observations about their voting habits, their civic activities, etc. Why don't you admit that it is precisely by utilizing such "quantitative" devices that we are able to pinpoint the "truly" objective$_2$ values in our government?

CRANSTON: Your problem is that you're looking for exactitude and pre-cision where none can be found. The viable and authentic, or objective$_2$, values in a society can never be determined by taking a "nose count." You can't employ a quantitative criterion to judge something that is essentially qualitative. The weakness of your position becomes especially evident when one group or faction within a government vies with others for the possession of the title to "the authentic moral standpoint." If by the use of quantitative measurements you succeeded in showing that the values of one particular faction were the strongest in that society, you would still not have succeeded in showing that these values were objective$_2$.

TURNER: Why not, if they supply the chief standards for behavior in that society?

CRANSTON: Simply because might is not right. I think I can pose the problem I am concerned about most clearly if we consider a situation where one "public morality" comes into conflict or contradiction with another. Consider the case of the Nazis: We denounced their regime as immoral and even executed many of the leaders of that regime as "criminals" in the aftermath of World War II, on the basis of our own objective$_{1\&2}$ morality. Are you going to say that we had a right to bring an objective$_2$ moral judgement against the Nazis simply because our own objective$_1$ public morality, coupled with the fact that we won the war, gave us that right?[7] That seems arbitrary to the nth degree.

TURNER: In a case like this, the definition of "public morality" has to be broadened. It was not just the U.S. and Britain and U.S.S.R. and other combatant nations who issued this judgement, but the overwhelming majority in the world community at that time. They happened to find a consensus among themselves that certain things the Nazis did were despicable, and they acted and punished accordingly. If World War III broke out and some nation was eventually judged responsible for it, it would be the community of nations that flourished at that time that would determine the degree of guilt and fix the responsibility. I'm afraid that's how "objective$_{1\&2}$ morality" works.

CRANSTON: Are you really willing to accept this appeal to numbers as your final criterion for "objective$_2$ morality"?

TURNER: You should not forget or ignore the great advantage this approach has: It enables one who is properly tuned into prevailing national and international value systems, to know specifically what the objective$_1$ values are at any particular time, and to determine what the objective$_2$ values are which he must take into account in fashioning his own behavior. When we focus on the crisscrossing currents of individual values, the picture is very confusing; but when we concentrate on the larger scene, a definite profile of the primary and prevailing and important virtues or values of a people begins to take on shape in the midst of all this fog.

CRANSTON: This is absolute eclecticism. You start off borrowing a cup of sugar from Hegel, and now you end up borrowing two cups of flour from Plato.

TURNER: Plato? Oh, I see what you mean. That's true. You mean, of course his contention that it is only in the state that the virtues of a people are written in "large enough letters" to be recognized and distinguished and defined.[8] I happen to think he was right about that. If Plato is properly demythologized, we can still learn a lot from him.

CRANSTON: Following through on Plato's model, I suppose the vices of the people will be "writ large" in the state, as well as the virtues?

TURNER: That may be so. But here is where we have to go beyond Plato since he was considering just the case of one state and would not have any strong concept of a "world" community. I think that to make the final distinction of "vice" from "virtue" will be the lot of greater states or civilizations, or members of the criticized state who adhere in spirit to the foreign states or civilizations that they consider to be greater.

CRANSTON: Just tell me one thing: What if the $objective_{1\&2}$ world morality during one era is judged by the $objective_{1\&2}$ morality of a later era to be completely *immoral?* Wouldn't you say that *one* of these objective moralities *must* be wrong?

TURNER: In order to handle that, I'd have to broaden my definition of "public morality" even further. The final $objective_{1\&2}$ morality would simply be the final standards and values that outlived all the rest and prevailed to the end.

CRANSTON: I find the whole trend in your thinking incredible. You start off making a "numbers game" out of $objective_2$ morality, and now it becomes a race for time, as well.

TURNER: Is that so bad? Why should I talk about some morality that "should" have become incorporated in the world as a whole, but never did? Politics is the "art of the possible" – in morals, too. If there is some brand of morality that is too lofty for the people in the world at some particular time – well, sad to say, it just is never going to become $objective_1$ in that world and $objective_2$ to that world. There may just *be* some higher morality that could and should become incorporated in the world, but we are never going to know that it was suitable, feasible and possible for the world, unless and until it actually comes to exist and prevail $objectively_{1\&2}$ *in* the world.

CRANSTON: I was hoping that we would at least be able to agree that the determination of $objective_{1\&2}$ morality should be more qualitative than quantitative.

TURNER: I'm afraid your emphasis on "quality," although seemingly innocuous and even commendable, reflects a basically elitist attitude. Reference to the "majority" sounds crude and quantitative, but it has been the key to the phenomenal progress of liberal democracy in the last two centuries, and is, I think, the value that the world needs most right now. Let's call it the "world ethic."

CRANSTON: Our conversation has not been a complete loss. I think we could even issue a joint communique which would read something like this: "If some $objective_2$ morality exists, it appears *par excellence* in the $objectivity_1$ of the state and the community of nations."

TURNER: That's a hypothetical formulation[9] that I could subscribe to.

But, of course, it is clear by now that you and I would *intend* two different things in using one and the same formulation. You would affirm the antecedent (that "some objective$_2$ morality exists") and see this as some inner "potentially objective$_2$," morality which eventually comes to the surface in the objective$_1$ socio-political structures. I would agree in affirming the antecedent, but simply because I identify objective$_2$ morality precisely with objective$_1$ morality. And I would see objective$_{1\&2}$ morality in the larger structures as giving direction and formation to the citizens living within the confines of these structures.

CRANSTON: Do you realize that, although you have suggested quantitative means for determining citizen input in a government, you end up saying that the objectivity$_2$ of the objective$_1$ morality in that government does not *depend* in any way, shape or form on that input?

TURNER: I don't deny the obvious fact that objective$_1$ morality depends to some extent on this "input" for its *existence*: however, citizen input receives its own objectivity$_2$ in turn from the prevailing socio-political system, with its laws, customs, institutions, etc. – and *not* vice versa. As I mentioned, the case gets a little more complicated in a democracy, where the "public morality" decrees that citizen input is an objective$_2$ value. But the principle remains the same.

CRANSTON: You talk as if the citizens do not actually create a democracy.

TURNER: Of course they do, but it is only after it is established and stabilized that it gives objective$_2$ respectability to "democratic" values and activities.

CRANSTON: I sincerely hope you always have a good democratic government to lend objective$_2$ respectability to your values and activities ... Before we leave this topic, I think one final corollary problem should be broached: I think we have both been presupposing all along that the individuals in any society or political system would *express* their values or virtues in the objective$_1$ realm. But it is at least conceivable that some and even many individuals would *not* express themselves at all. Would you want to say that the individual has any obligation, any fundamental moral obligation, to express himself in *some* way in society at large? If not, then it could possibly happen, if everyone happened to be fugitive and recalcitrant, that there would be no society, and no objective$_{1 \text{ or } 2}$ morality.

TURNER: That could not possibly happen. The world, by the subtle and/or overt pressures and sanctions which it brings to bear on the behavior of individuals, will not only make it quite clear what are the important tenets of the objective$_{1\&2}$ morality, but will also employ appropriate pressures to persuade each individual to express his or her morality in *some* suitable way.

There may be some special inner attraction or inclination which leads people to find satisfaction in such expression. But an "inner obligation" dictating such expression would be superfluous. The world will promulgate and enforce in quite an external way all the obligations that are necessary to achieve the desired end.

CHAPTER VI

LEGALITY AND MORALITY

In the differences of private men, to declare what is ... moral virtue, and to make [it] binding, there is need of the ordinances of sovereign power, and punishments to be ordained for such as shall break them; which ordinances are therefore part of the civil law.

Thomas Hobbes,[1] *Leviathan* II, 26

What is a good law? By a *good law*, I mean not a just law: for no law can be unjust. The law is made by the sovereign power, and all that is done by such power is warranted and owned by every one of the people ... A good law is that which is needful, for the good of the people, and withal perspicuous ...

Thomas Hobbes, *Leviathan* II, 30

I think it is clear that the criminal law as we know it is based upon moral principle. In a number of crimes its function is simply to enforce a moral principle and nothing else ... There are no theoretical limits to the power of the State to legislate against treason and sedition, and likewise I think there can be no theoretical limits to legislation against immorality ... Immorality ..., for the purpose of the law, is what every right-minded person is presumed to consider to be immoral ... Nothing should be punished by the law that does not lie beyond the limits of tolerance. It is not nearly enough to say that a majority dislike a practice: there must be a real feeling of reprobation ... [The presence of disgust] is a good indication that the bounds of toleration are being reached ... The morals which underly the law must be derived from the sense of right and wrong which resides in the community as a whole ... As far as possible. however, privacy should be respected.

Lord Patrick Devlin,[2] "The Enforcement of Morals," Maccabaean Lecture in Jurisprudence, British Academy, 1959

CRANSTON: I thought about the above passages from Hobbes as you were expatiating in our last discussion on the objective$_{1\&2}$ determination of morality by the "powers that be." Do you admit to a more than coincidental similarity?

TURNER: I agree with Hobbes in some respects. For one thing, he made the very important point that the term, "morality," is applicable in a strict and objective sense only to those qualities which facilitate the constructive and harmonious intercommunication and interaction of human beings – I guess you would prefer to call this "*social* morality." At any rate, once one focuses on this area as the main target in moral standard-setting, it becomes obvious that society or the state has a fundamental and very crucial role in determining the morals of the people. This is why Hobbes goes on to say, "no law can be unjust." For the law as an objective$_2$ standard of justice for the people, cannot be measured or judged by those whom it is measuring and judging. As long as these laws are promulgated and enforced, they provide during that time the ultimate norms for rectitude and justice for a people. As Hobbes points out, this does not necessarily mean they are "good." They might be tyrannical, badly framed, or superfluous. But if they're in force, they're "just" ...

This being said, I should point out that there is also a major difference between the sort of thing I was saying, and what Hobbes says. It should be clear by now that I favor democratic institutions and procedures, while Hobbes was an adamant monarchist and was thinking about a single absolute sovereign legislating the morals of his subjects – something that the public morality that we both subscribe to would frown upon, and designate as "immoral."

CRANSTON: Getting back to the 20th century – does that other statement, by Lord Devlin, sound any more "democratic" to your ears?

TURNER: It's very strange how much attention that address to the British Academy has been receiving lately, in spite of the fact that it's hardly an elaborate and extremely original piece of ethical thinking. Perhaps the best way to explain the interest it caused would be to utilize your own beloved category of an "idea whose time has come." The idea "whose time has come," in this case, was the relaxation of laws against certain "private" offenses. The particular *cause celebré* which supplied the fuel for Delvin's fire was the recommendation of a government committee that the laws against homosexuality be relaxed. Devlin at this point became the distinguished spokesman for the conservative reaction whose arousal was natural and inevitable. People were bound to ask, sooner or later, "how can the government say that immorality is outside the jurisdiction of the law"? And when they said "immorality," they might have in mind homosexuality or prostitution, or the buying or selling of pornography, or abortion. Once you admitted the principle that these "offenses" were immune to legislation because they were matters of *private* morals, a long list of corollaries also followed suit: euthanasia, suicide, incest, duelling, etc. People began to realize all these implications, and so the intellectual polarization which Devlin's paper elicited is readily understandable ... But getting back to your last question: No, I don't identify with Devlin's reaction, but rather I think it's a good example of the way conservative elements in a democratic milieu would try to counteract what they consider to be a massive trend toward moral permissiveness or laxity.

CRANSTON: I don't want to attribute "guilt by association," but you *do* seem to identify with Devlin in your defense of society and the state as a final authority in morality. In particular, I recall that you pointed to a kind of "majority rule" in democratic societies as the final determinant of the objective morality. And it seems to me that your utilitarian emphasis on the "greatest happiness for the greatest number" exemplifies a tendency in the same general direction.

TURNER: It's one thing to maintain (as I have) that "objective morality" in a democracy is conditioned by majority input, and quite another to say that this objective morality should become a matter of *law*. Now, it is hardly conceivable that a judicious employment of "my" utilitarian criterion could lead to the consensus that something like homosexuality is "objectively immoral"; but even if there were such a consensus, it would not necessarily have to be expressed in laws and legal action. At this point, it is important to make a distinction between the somewhat negative and coercive aspects of the "public morality" and the positive and/or persuasive aspects. There are many extra-legal and non-coercive ways of promulgating and "enforcing" a public morality – by ignoring offenders, denying them jobs, gossiping about them, and rewarding non-offenders in all sorts of subtle or not-so-subtle ways. *Laws* should only be brought to bear on certain types of behavior which are obviously dangerous to the existence and welfare of society, and which need to be backed up with appropriately strong criminal sanctions. Examples would be murder and theft. "Offences" such as homosexuality and abortion pose such a small threat to the commonweal that they are obviously in "another ballpark" altogether.

I think a good example of the two different types of sanctions employed by the "public morality" is found in Nixon's statement in his famous "Checker's speech" in the 50's, that "It isn't a question of whether (my behavior) was legal or illegal. That isn't enough. The question is, was it morally wrong?" As a politician, he was quite aware that he had to conform not merely to the laws on the books, which backed up the more dramatic offenses against the "public morality" with stipulated punishments, but also to the unwritten but omnipresent standards of public decency, norms which, for a politician were backed up with an especially appropriate sanction (disgrace and/or removal from public office). These "unwritten standards" are a motley group of things in any culture. They may include customs, traditions, matters of etiquette, things you don't do even in private, things you can do but should not get caught at, etc. A great mass of these things will never become subject to official legislation. Now it is unfortunately possible that something like homosexuality may become subject to censure from the"unofficial" department of the public morality, but it would be ridiculous to make official laws about such acts, and to try to back up these laws with due sanctions.

CRANSTON: I think your separation of official laws from customs, manners, etc. is just a bit too neat. Judges and jurists in some particular society may have unwritten "customs" in *interpreting* and applying the law, which are more important than the laws themselves. Do you want to add these "customs" as a new and separate category relating to the enforcement of "public morality?"

TURNER: I don't want to make a learned distinction of all the various spheres of public morality – branch A, branch B, etc. But your point is well-taken. It is possible that the sanctions that seem to be determined by the "law" are actually regulated by unwritten "customs" of the sort you mention.

CRANSTON: Would you agree with Devlin that, *if* there is a vast consensus in society that offenses like homosexuality are "disgusting," this provides sufficient grounds for society to make appropriate laws-with-sanctions assuring that society's happiness will not be infringed on?

TURNER: That's an idiotic idea. How is society harmed by the private sexual practices of consenting adult homosexuals? If society is not threatened by such practices, no preventive legislation is justified. As I said before, laws are only appropriate where there are *serious threats* to the peace, welfare, happiness, etc. of society. That is certainly not the case here. I'm surprised that an experienced judge like Devlin would be willing to define and apply such frivolous laws as laws prohibiting homosexuality.

CRANSTON: You miss his point entirely. It is not important whether you *or* Devlin consider an offense like homosexuality a serious threat to your happiness. The question is, what if a consensus exists as a matter of fact in society as a whole, that such acts are serious threats to the happiness of the majority. Does not *such* a society have a right to legislate against the acts in question?

TURNER: A right? I don't determine or give them such a right. If they utilized the proper and accepted channels to enact legislation concerning private morals, then I suppose one would have to say that their legislation becomes an exemplification of "public morality." But I personally don't think such legislation would be justified (and lasting, as well) unless they could show in some way or another that a real threat was actually being posed by such behavior. And I don't see how they could establish this.

CRANSTON: Isn't this hypothetical society really using good utilitarian criteria in its own way? I mean, the citizens are basing their evaluation on projected consequences which they deem to be important to them and their happiness. *You* do not perceive the same consequences ensuing, but that does not necessarily mean *they* are wrong. How can you fault the procedure they are using to justify their attitude?

TURNER: They might be going through the motions of applying utilitarian criteria, but only the motions. Let me give an example: If I were to use a quasi-Kantian test like, "is the maxim of your action universalizable, so as to bring the greatest happiness to the greatest number"? – it would *sound* like utilitarianism but would in reality be compromised by the universalizability test. The reason for this is that if we really universalized in a Kantian spirit, we would have to forget about happiness altogether – as Kant himself insists.

CRANSTON: You've already said it is impossible to universalize in the Kantian way, so why talk about it now as if it were possible?

TURNER: I just mention this as an example of a self-contradiction. You can't use a rule which depends on consequences for assessing something which is not a consequence at all, but the antithesis of a consequence. I am thinking of the example you gave of the offense people take at homosexuality. The offense they feel is not caused by the homosexuality, which is quite private, but rather it is the case that their own disgust (a subjective attitude) is the *cause* of the existence of the "offense" that they are reacting to.

CRANSTON: I'll have to work on that a bit ... Can you perceive of *any* sort of circumstances in which you would consider legislation against homosexuality warranted?

TURNER: Of course. If a state had a potential revolution on its hands because of the strong feelings of the citizenry against homosexuals, the state might have no option but to give into the citizens' demands, however irrational they might seem to be. I'm thinking particularly of a democratic state, in which the desires and demands of the people are supposed to be reflected in the laws and the machinery of government.

CRANSTON: That example is a bit "far out."

TURNER: Let's put a better face on the example: Let's say that in a particular society, lynching and all manner of violence is practiced against homosexuals. In such a situation, the state might legislate against homosexuality just to sublimate all this violence, and protect the lives and property of homosexuals by offering them "due process" of the law.

CRANSTON: That scenario is still a bit on the dramatic side. Let us say in a more everyday vein that the people in a particular society consider homosexuality a threat to the institution of marriage. Would it be frivolous and capricious of them to demand laws against homosexuality, to protect this institution which, you must admit, has some fundamental importance for the maintenance and progress of "society" as we now know it?

TURNER: I'm stretching my imagination to the fullest, and all I can perceive is a purely imaginary "affront" to heterosexual eugamic society by a homosexual's individual pursuit of sexual fulfillment. If you add to this the fact that recent studies[3] indicate a definite physiological-hormonal cause for homosexuality (a certain ratio of etiocholanolane to androsterone in the urine) the case becomes even stronger. How can you penalize people for their basic physical makeup? If the number of homosexuals grows, and if homosexuality is something purely physical, *let* marriage flounder and fail. Institutions in our society at least, are supposed to be for the promotion of happiness of individuals. If they don't do that, get rid of the institutions.

CRANSTON: What if the causes of homosexuality were shown to be definitely psychological or psychosocial rather than physical, would this lead you to shift in your stand?

TURNER: Not unless, as I already indicated, a civil crisis of major proportions was looming. But I seriously doubt whether such a psychological etiology could be shown. Psychologists are not much more proficient than philosophers when it comes to establishing such concrete "facts."

CRANSTON: At this point I think it might be appropriate to point out that a *predominately* homosexual society would hardly last many generations.

TURNER: Very well, then, let us say "amen" to the biological laws. All this means is that we don't need any special societal laws to assure the extinction of homosexuals. Heterosexual society can win by default, by just allowing homosexuals to "do their own thing." If the heterosexuals are just patient, they're bound to end up as a majority again. And everybody, during the interim, will be sexually fulfilled. A very nice fairy-tale ending, don't you think?

CRANSTON: "Fairy-tale" is right. I suppose the ogre for the heterosexuals in this little story would be a giant called "Birth Control"? ... While you were weaving your tale, however, you seemed to slur over some very concrete practical problems about homosexuality that often occur to the minds of heterosexuals. I am thinking in particular of an alleged threat to the safety of young children from unscrupulous marauding adult homosexuals.

TURNER: With that, I think you have hit on the crux of the whole "homosexual" problem. Even when people talk in general terms about being "disgusted" with homosexuality, they have something like this in mind. They are really thinking about the possibility that their sons or daughters, because of early exposure to homosexual "carriers," would grow up with that dread disease which prevents sons and daughters from perpetuating their family name and fortune. They cry out "immorality!" but they are really thinking how regrettable it would be if heterosexual fathers and mothers weren't able to have children (and grandchildren) like themselves. This is a good example of the way in which the individual "sense of duty" that you would like to champion, becomes irresponsible and irrational ... But, in answer to your question, even if it could be shown that there was some threat to the safety or welfare of youngsters from homosexuals, this would afford no more justification for officially outlawing homosexuality, than the potential threat of pedophiles to young girls is justification for outlawing adult *hetero*sexuality.

CRANSTON: I take it that the only situation in which you would approve of anti-homosexual laws would be one in which homosexualtiy was definitely proven to be physically and psychologically avoidable, and gave rise to some sort of an extreme social crisis or potential revolution?

TURNER: In a case like that, the people would actually be "proving" by their agitation that homosexuality was socially "dangerous." It would be a sort of self-fulfilling prophecy initiated by organized anti-homosexuals. In the face of such "proof," the lawmaker would probably have no choice but to outlaw homosexuality, at least for a while, until the whole thing blew over.

CRANSTON: It goes without saying that you have a very pragmatic view of the law. For you, it's just something there to maintain essential social relations, and prevent drastic social mishaps. You do not envision the law as having even indirect jurisdiction over people's thoughts, feelings, moral or immoral intentions.

TURNER: That's correct.

CRANSTON: And yet, doesn't the law itself belie your characterization of it? I mean, doesn't the law place considerable emphasis on a person's intentions, in judging criminal responsibility? In our Western legal systems, the principle of *mens rea* is taken for granted in almost all cases: A person can't be judged guilty of a crime unless it can be established that he intended to commit the crime, and was morally responsible for it. If the law really operates in the pragmatic way that you have been adumbrating, isn't the law itself rather inconsistent in looking for evidence of personal moral intentions, in making decisions about convictions?

TURNER: You are wrong if you consider *mens rea* to be a universal attribute of the laws. There are a growing number of laws on the books which specify "strict" liability, i.e. any person who breaks the law will receive such-and-such punishment if he is caught, no matter *what* his intentions were. But even where *mens rea* prevails, it doesn't really *mean* that the subjective moral intentions of an offender have any primacy at all. If, for example, there is overwhelming factual evidence that someone has tried to assassinate the President of the United States, but it can be shown that he or she really felt a strong personal moral *duty* to carry out the assassination attempt – the judge and jury will yawn and come out with a conviction and sentence anyway. They might even stiffen the sentence on the basis that people with such unusual moral convictions are more dangerous to society than ordinary criminals.

CRANSTON: But you have to admit that moral intentions are very often considered mitigating or exonerating factors, when officials apply various laws. For instance, conscientious objectors have generally been treated more leniently in our society than out-and-out draft evaders. Since their offense is essentially the same, what other explanation is there for the difference in treatment, if not that some very subjective reasons of conscience were taken into account in both cases, and were found to have differing degrees of "acceptibility" or "heinousness," however you look at it?

TURNER: Certainly, to all appearances, it looks as if the subjective aspects became a major or even *the* major factor in such cases. But the appearances are deceptive. What really happens is this: Society sets up laws to prevent people from doing certain things which it considers particularly dangerous or anti-social. But in judging alleged offenders, it often makes a very understandable distinction between mere injury, on the one hand, and insult-plus-injury on the other hand. If individual A has transgressed the proper limits, but shows regret and goes out of his way to give acceptable justifying reasons for the transgression, society will be inclined to be more lenient with him. If individual B not only transgresses those limits, but adds insult to injury by showing that he doesn't even care about the fact that the limits were there, or even by showing that he *enjoyed* the act of transgression – society gets rowled up even more and very likely metes out a more severe penalty. In such cases, society is not actually judging the "intentions," but the external signs the individual gives of indifference or contempt or malicious enjoyment. The impression is that a person who gives these signs will be in all probability harder to keep in line, and may require tighter restrictions. So you see, society is still applying a pragmatic criterion. There is no real concern about the subjective moral state of the offending individual, except insofar as certain practical *consequences* are foreseen or projected as resulting from this subjective state.

CRANSTON: Applying your pragmatic criterion, is there no way of avoiding the situation where society's reaction (in the form of legal restraints) is based on purely imaginary pseudo-consequences of offenders' behavior, rather than real or realistically projected consequences?

TURNER: I'm afraid not. If there is some society with unbalanced sensitivity and outlandishly intense feelings, they may want to legislate on the basis of their fears rather than on the basis of real dangers. And there is nothing we can do to stop them.

CRANSTON: And so, "the majority rules" in law as well as in morals. This seems to me to be the most objectionable aspect of your utilitarian way of thinking. Isn't there a moral obligation to include or exclude certain things in the law, *regardless* of how the majority feels? What if (for example) a given society saw fit to legalize the perpetration of violence upon some disfavored minority, to abrogate the property rights of that minority and nullify all contractual rights that they might have? Certainly such laws are *unjust* no matter how the majority feels and what reasons they may give for their feelings.

TURNER: Your example is well-chosen. If you had spoken about legalizing violence towards *everyone* in that society, and abrogating everyone's property rights and contractual claims, I think it would be obvious that such a society would "self-destruct" and be so short-lived that it would offer graphic and living proof of the injustice of its laws. But when you're speaking about the legal rights of a *minority*, the case is not so clear-cut. It's quite possible for a society to adopt discriminatory legislation with regard to a minority, and yet endure and thrive. And if the majority in that society were challenged to justify their attitude. I'm sure they could point out all sorts of "dangers" entailed by giving too much freedom to the disfavored minority, and catastrophic consequences that would result if the discriminatory laws were modified.

CRANSTON: A case in point is the discriminatory laws or discriminatory applications of laws against blacks that have prevailed in the northern as well as the southern U.S. for so long, even after the emancipation proclamation. Wouldn't it have been feasible and commendable for some statesman or legislator to buck the trend and, *in the name of justice*, modify the laws in favor of the minority.

TURNER: It is inconceivable that some single political official might have such power in a democracy. Under our system, the main possibility for protection of minority rights lies with the Supreme Court. The Supreme Court justices have the power to effectively nullify discriminatory laws, and *de facto* many of the major discriminatory laws which have been changed, have been changed as a result of the Supreme Court whittling away at them little by little. But the justices, like all governmental officials, have to read the "signs of the time" and await the proper moment for such decisions. If the recent court decisions in favor of equal educational rights and equal voting rights for minorities had been made at the turn of the century they would have either been ignored or led to debilitating violence, instability or even revolution in the nation. Such an early and premature decision would, certainly, have been an expression of the personal ideas about "justice" entertained by the majority of justices, but the prevailing concepts about justice would supersede their decisions and perhaps even lead to the dismantling of the power of the Supreme Court.

CRANSTON: One thing you seem to be forgetting amidst all these expatiations is the tremendous educational efficacy of the laws. The laws not only reflect the prevailing morality, but help to inculcate and propagate certain moral values. You don't seem to realize that the legislators and jurists, if they have any superior wisdom at all, very often have to preempt the political processes that lead to modification of the laws, in order to give direction to that great mass of people who don't think for themselves but only follow current trends. Even a popularly-elected representative must come at certain times to a crossroads of decision where he must cease to reflect the wishes of his constituents and take on the role of directing these wishes and, in short, "educating" his constituents.

TURNER: There's a lot of dispute about the proper role of an "elected representative." But never mind that. I'm on your side. I believe the laws have such an educative function. I think the only thing we would disagree on would be the matter of the proper timing of "educative" laws. The "Emancipation Proclamation" probably had a desirable educational effect during the time of Lincoln, because the majority were just about ready for it. There was, for instance, a lot of jealousy on the part of the labor force in the North at the time because of the cheap slave labor which was fattening the coffers of Southern plantation owners and industrialists. This, combined with other factors, made the presidential proclamation a timely decision. But if it had been issued a few decades previous to Lincoln's term of office, at a time when the majority were not even beginning to discover that slavery did not contribute to *their* happiness, the results would have been nil and certainly non-educational, and the conservative reaction might have forestalled the possibility of emancipation for an even longer period of time. Now, this necessity of waiting and waiting for the proper time before laws can become just *and* operative *and* educative, may be one of the defects of a democracy. As Aristotle observed a long time ago, democracy on a large scale can be a rather slow and ungainly form of government when it is a question of inaugurating reforms. But, as a form of government, it also has many assets.

CRANSTON: Speaking of this "slowness" of democracy, it seems obvious to me that one of the chief "retardants" to the cause of legal justice in a democracy is that very utilitarian ethic which you espouse so avidly. I don't doubt that a utilitarian ethic in some form or other reflects the prevailing value system in this country. But, as has been dramatically demonstrated by our long history of discriminatory laws against minorities – concern for the "greatest good of the *greatest number*" is not enough. If we are to give more than lip-service to "equal treatment for *all*," we must use our laws to enforce some higher standard than utilitarianism.

TURNER: You do an injustice to utilitarianism. Utilitarianism is just about the highest ethic that could be incorporated into, or expressed by, the laws. Civil and criminal laws are, after all, "*minimal* regulations." They tell people what minimal standards they have to meet if they want to avoid public censure and official infringement on their own happiness. It's quite a progressive step forward to get the majority of people of a vast nation to agree even that the laws should contribute to the welfare *of the majority*. To expect the average citizen to go beyond that and opt constantly and consistently for equal treatment of *all*, is beyond the ken and capabilities of *any* system of law.

CRANSTON: Communists and socialists claim to be oriented primarily toward such absolute equality.

TURNER: And they end up, in actual fact, with new privileged classes and types of systematic discrimination that the non-socialist would have never even thought of before.

CRANSTON: What you seem to be saying is that the ideal of "equal treatment under the law" is an unrealizable myth. But whence did it come? How do you explain the fact that it is such an important principle in our ethical and legal thinking now?

TURNER: Some say that it derives from Christian ideas – the notion that all men are brothers, all creatures of God, all equally sinful without the grace of God, and so forth. I think its origin might possibly be explained in that way. At any rate, as a religious ideal, it's a "maximal regulation" – an ultimate mark or goal that people might aim at. But, like the Christian maxim about "loving all mankind," it is forever unrealizable and certainly cannot be completely provided for either by a legal system or a viable moral code.

CRANSTON: I presume you consider utilitarianism a "minimal" code of moral behavior.

TURNER: It's minimal, but, on the other hand, it's about as maximal as an *ethical* rule can get, without becoming quixotic and inefficacious. I might say that it's *the maximal* "minimal moral norm."

CRANSTON: But it's still minimal, and so perhaps there is a real need for religion with *unequivocally* maximal norms, to offset all these "minimal" orientations, and lead with the greatest celerity to a non-discriminatory and highly educative legal system.

TURNER: Religion may try to do that, and I suppose charismatic religious leaders have often tried to do just that.

CRANSTON: But you have to admit, religion has a real educative *problem* if the laws and customs of a society are extremely inimical to its "maximal" recommendations, and in fact are teaching an absolutely contrary minimal "doctrine."

TURNER: That may be religion's problem right now. But (as the long and seamy history of mankind has shown) even greater problems are likely to emerge if the laws of the state are used to enforce some religion and its codes.

CRANSTON: Then we have here an example of an educative problem that is theoretically solvable by religion, except that the use of religion might give rise to even weightier problems than the ones it is meant to solve.

TURNER: How very, very true. You see, we don't have to disagree all the time.

CRANSTON: Control your optimism. That's a tentative concession, not necessarily an agreement ... I guess the main thing that bothers me about your whole way of thinking, is that you seem to see no problem at all in private immorality. In fact, it hardly seems to exist for you.

TURNER: If there is such a thing as private immorality, why should it concern me and you? The very fact that it is *private* precludes my being affected by it, and is a good reason for not trying to make laws governing it.

CRANSTON: And yet it seems self-evident to me that if a substantial number of the members of some society were practicing some form of "private immorality," the unity and perdurance of that society would be seriously endangered.

TURNER: This is a turnabout. You began by accusing me of dictating morality externally like Devlin, but it seems you would like to enforce some moral norms legally, just like Devlin.

CRANSTON: In logic, that's called the *ad verecundiam* fallacy[4] ... I would suggest that we consider a problem that Devlin did not give much attention to – abortion. (I think this issue provides the most substantial contemporary challenge to the reputed indifference of laws to matters of private morality.) I suppose that, if it could be shown that the unborn fetus was human, it would be clear that abortion amounted to murder, and it would be easy to get legislation against abortion. I mean, the big question that makes abortion seem a "private" rather than a "public" matter, is this difficulty in determining whether the fetus is a *person*.

TURNER: That's not exactly the issue. The crucial question is whether the fetus is a "*legal* person."[5] And the answer to that is, that under our present legal system it certainly is *not*. That is precisely why anti-abortion laws are falling by the wayside now, one by one.

CRANSTON: What about those of us who happen to disagree with the merely legal definitions of "person"? Must we simply accept what the law says as the "last word," and consider the matter closed? Are you going to tell me that, in spite of the fact that a *substantial* number of citizens still believe the fetus is a person, what one does to the fetus is not to be considered murder, because the law does not call it that.

TURNER: The law is an expression of the public morality. If it were a tenet of the public morality that the fetus is a person, you can be pretty sure that the prevailing laws against murder would be applied in full force in abortion cases. The fact that this is *not* happening leads one to believe that abortion must be relegated to the sphere of private morality.

CRANSTON: You deny, then, that abortion is murder?

TURNER: I don't know. Abortion may be homicide. I suppose if the fetus is a person it *is* homicide. But that's not the point, anyway. The point is, even if it is homicide, it's purely *private* homicide. I know this sounds cold, callous and unsympathetic, but it's a fact we have to deal with. If this is homicide, it's apparently a type of homicide that doesn't affect or threaten the existence of most citizens in our society. If it did, there wouldn't be such ambivalence about it, society would call it "murder" purely and simply, and there would be laws or strong social sanctions against it.

CRANSTON: It seems to me that there *are* strong social sanctions against it right now. People disapprove of it, and are expressing their disapproval of it in various ways, including petitioning for prohibitory laws.

Let me subject you to a very specific test, which I think should be useful in bringing out the implications of your position. Imagine that you are a legislator who happens to be firmly convinced that abortion is, indeed, murder. Now, the people in your constituency seem to be about equally divided – the number of letters you receive both pro and con on the legalization of abortion is just about equal. In view of what we've called the "educative" aspects of legislation, wouldn't you feel justified in tipping the scales a bit in the "con" direction, instead of taking a neutral or even a "pro" position?

TURNER: As a legislator, my main motive in the making of criminal laws would be to deter crime. If I am privately unsympathetic to abortion, but can see no great threat to public safety or welfare from it, I have no right to "tip the scales," as you say. In fact, in this particular example, when one conjurs up the spectre of abortion mills and unsanitary underground operations, and the resultant maternal deaths, it becomes obvious that the *greatest* threat to the public safety and welfare comes from the *prohibition* of abortion rather than its legalization.

CRANSTON: I can see that my little test has at least succeeded in bringing out what is probably the prime consideration in the mind of pro-abortion legislators.

TURNER: Perhaps. But I think you may be placing too much emphasis altogether on the legislative end of things. The real vanguard in changing the laws on abortion has been comprised of *jurists* rather than legislators. It is the jurists who, by selecting what cases are to come up, what precedents are significant, what evidence is to be admitted, and what procedures are appropriate in appealing cases – seem to be the "culprits," here, if you want to call them that. The legislators more or less "bring up the rear."

CRANSTON: That's a good point, but it seems to favor my own contention: I mean, jurists certainly do not have the same obligation as legislators to reflect to some degree the wishes of their electors, and their function is not to make general laws but to interpret the laws and apply them to individuals, or at least to specific cases. It seems to me that the jurist may certainly have more leeway in consulting and acting in accord with his own "private" moral convictions than the legislator. For instance, a judge in adjudicating an abortion case may choose to weigh the purported pejorative social effects of illegal abortion against certain intangible factors, such as the spiritual damage suffered by an abortionist or voluntarily aborted woman, the possible distortion of the personality of a doctor or mother who even once engages in an act which shows a gross disrespect for human life – and so forth.

TURNER: As a moral "jurist," I think you've set up this "case" in such a way as to favor a pet thesis of yours. That's called "conflict of interest."

CRANSTON: I hope you don't mean to imply that a judge must ignore matters of conscience and very subjective moral responsibilities when he is making his decisions. If so, I would refer you to the concept of "equity" which has become a very important feature of the English and American judicial systems.[6] In accord with "equity," processes have been set up in each system for allowing certain judicial authorities to override and make exceptions to the laws, in the interest of strictly moral considerations or insight into the "natural law."

TURNER: I have my doubts about how "subjective" a judgement in equity could be, and still stand unchallenged. But I will not dispute the fact that judges do and even should supplement the laws with what might be called "moral" judgements. It is also possible that some such considerations might come into play in the judgement of an abortion case – although I can't imagine offhand how this would come about. But at any rate, in your own considerations you have forgotten about one very important factor that would certainly be taken into account by any judge that gets a case like this nowadays: namely, the need of making efficient use of law enforcement personnel. It would seem almost absurd to keep law enforcement officers running after pregnant women and recalcitrant doctors, when there is already insufficient manpower to prevent more serious crimes like murder and armed robbery, or even track down and punish the offenders; and when the court dockets are filled to overflowing with untried cases and our prisons are bulging at the seams from overpopulation problems. I hate to bring in such utterly mundane considerations. But, in a way, the "law" which we revere so much is a very mundane instrument – suited only for maintaining a certain reasonable equilibrium between good and evil in society, and keeping anti-social actions from getting out of hand. Judges who would try to use the law to back up their own moral nostrums, may end up causing a lot of innocent people to get mugged or knifed because of the supererogatory diversions they are introducing into the laws, and/or putting an intolerable strain on the whole law enforcement apparatus.

CRANSTON: To a certain extent, what you say is true, but only because citizens are unwilling to support law enforcement activities and the judicial system beyond the bare minimum necessary for the protection of life and limb.

TURNER: Well, then, that is a sad fact that both you and I must deal with. And I think it is highly probable that even a person like yourself who has moral objections to abortion, would be willing to legalize it, or at least to refrain from trying to enforce laws against it, if he seriously considers some seemingly insignificant and merely statistical "fact" such as this.

CRANSTON: It occurs to me that perhaps Lord Devlin's remarks have to be interpreted as referring to an ideal world. I mean, it would be ideal and indisputably desirable that the laws in a given society should coincide with the consciences and private moral aspirations of the citizens.

TURNER: An "ideal" world, to my mind, connotes a world in which citizens do not get all worked up about unrealistic or utopian moral ideals.

CRANSTON: I suppose you would like every individual citizen, before allowing any of his "private" aspirations to come to full bloom, to do a quick check to see whether it conforms to the prevailing "objective morality" and is, or could be made into, a law.

TURNER: Does that sound overly pragmatic and compromising to you? I'm afraid it's the only way Devlin (and you) are ever going to attain the sort of "harmony" of morality and law that you're hankering after. If individuals don't have sufficient tolerance and social sensitivity to go through a process something like this, society must necessarily tend towards a very repressive brand of conservatism. Everyone will want to insist that some traditional but outmoded "truth" that they learned from their parents or in catechism class, be incorporated into the fibers of public law.

CRANSTON: It's funny that you should speak of conservatism in a pejorative sense here, because it seems to me that your own position is the epitome of conservatism.[7] In a society where individuals have to caucus and take an opinion poll and calculate the statistics on possible consequences every time they get the urge to support the legalization of a moral ideal, moral "progress" will be doomed to proceeding at a very phlegmatic pace.

TURNER: So do you really think a radical with fiery mien and far-out ideas is going to have some long-range progressive effects on the society which tolerates him?

What you have labeled as "conservatism" here is really the way that *practical* progressive people are going to get their "moral aspirations" eventually incorporated into the public morality and the law, while the idealists with their private nostrums stand by the sidelines and wonder what is happening.

CHAPTER VII

ATHEISM AND ETHICS

No one who in obedience to the laws believed that there were
Gods, ever intentionally did any unholy act, or uttered an un-
lawful word, but those who did must have supposed one of
three things – either that (the Gods) did not exist, which is the
first possibility, or secondly, that if they did, they took no care
of man, or thirdly, that they were easily appeased and turned
aside from their purpose by sacrifices and prayers.

The Athenian-Stranger, in Plato's *Laws*,X

Those are not all to be tolerated who deny the being of a God.
Promises, covenants, and oaths, which are the bonds of human
society, can have no hold upon an atheist. The taking away of
God, though but even in thought, dissolves all ...

John Locke, *A Letter Concerning Toleration*

It's magnificent, Alyosha, this science! A new [scientific]man's
arising – that I understand ... What will become of men ...
without God and immortal life? All things are lawful then, [and
men] can do what they like?

Dmitri speaking to Alyosha, in Dostoev-
sky's *The Brothers Karamazov*

CRANSTON: In our previous discussions, we have been trying to consider
morality as a sphere independent of religion. This mental separation of the
two spheres may be necessary to a certain extent, to facilitate philosophical
treatment of the subject. But on the other hand, it may be a mistake to carry
the separation too far. If the authors I've quoted above are correct, the real
and practical (as opposed to theoretical) separation of religion from morality
may have disastrous consequences for morality.

TURNER: I don't dismiss that possibility completely. An observation like
that seems particularly relevant to the sort of culture that Plato was living
in and commenting on: religion and ethical thinking were so inseparably
intertwined at that time that deficiency in religious belief could almost be

taken as an infallible token of a departure from accepted moral norms. This, of course, is one reason why the Greek authorities were so upset by Socrates' apparent disregard for the traditional polytheistic religious beliefs. They thought that if Socrates were allowed to continue, and if there were others like him, that their system couldn't continue. As it turned out, they were mistaken about Socrates' reputed atheism.[1] And Plato, in defending the place of religion in the ideal state, would certainly want to make room for the more advanced and ideal theism that Socrates espoused. But the basic perception that religious beliefs were intimately related to acceptable moral behavior, was no doubt quite true then.

But as philosophy and ethics have become more and more independent of religion, that perception has become less and less valid and relevant. I don't mean to say that ethics has finally attained independence. Much of the prevailing normative ethics in our culture has its source in our religions. And I think Locke's admonition and Dmitri's statement in *Brothers Karamazov* illustrate the sort of fears that still postpone our ethical "declaration of independence" from religion. It's another example of a "conservative reaction."[2]

CRANSTON: I take it that you are confident that philosophy is going to be able to eventually develop a normative ethics that can "stand on its own two feet"?

TURNER: I really think that is coming. But it requires a lot more ground-breaking of a metaethical sort[3] before it can become an accomplished fact. For example, we have to determine more precisely what is meant by "right" and "good," and whether and how moral statements can be judged as true or false, before we can get down to the nitty gritty of making true and meaningful statements about what is right and wrong.

CRANSTON: And what do we do in the meantime, while the philosophers are still slugging it out, trying to determine whether we can make true ethical statements, etc.?

TURNER: We do just what we have been doing – recommending normative[4] ethical maxims such as the utilitarian rule, which I have been defending. It would be nice, of course, if we could justify such rules more perfectly; but in the absence of that sort of justification, we have to go on living.

CRANSTON: And what if, by chance, the metaethicists should discover to their chagrin that moral statements can never be justified or falsified. Will you continue to make them anyway?

TURNER: I'm afraid that could never happen. It would be like proving the non-existence of God. It's one thing to prove a positive assertion, or refute some positive assertion; it's quite another to establish some absolute negative

assertion that would take an infinite amount of experience to prove beyond
the shadow of a doubt. Just as the judicious agnostic has to face the unlikely
fact that he is likely somewhere, sometime to encounter some proof for
God's existence that he won't be able to falsify, so also the cautious metaethicist has to be resigned to the far-out possibility that he might someday
come across a normative ethical assertion that can be proven and justified.

CRANSTON: Sounds like a real tread-mill existence. In the meantime, while
the metaethicians are feverishly searching for the key to deciphering and
validating ethical statements, don't you think it might help if normative
ethics got a little boost now and then from religious beliefs?

TURNER: I'm not so sure that that will help. In fact, it might serve to
postpone and even prevent the final emancipation of normative ethics. The
son who is still "holding on to his mother's apron strings," and is thinking
about becoming independent, has to actually make a break for it to become
independent. If he thinks he is going to first become independent and *then*
make his break, he is hampered by an impractical and idealistic "timetable."

CRANSTON: Do you really think normative ethics can become completely
free of theistic presuppositions, that morality can flourish just as well or
better without the help of theistic beliefs, as with that help?

TURNER: You seem to make those questions synonymous, but they are
two separate questions: It is conceivable *a)* that ethics could become an
autonomous master-*science* without this necessarily causing *b)* any change
for the better in the "morality" of *people*. But I doubt that that would happen.
So I would answer "yes" to both questions.

I would like to bring one thing to your attention here: You are speaking
of "theism" as if it were always something good and beneficial. But Plato
himself makes the point that it makes a big difference what *kind* of God one
believes in: If one believes in a God who just sits up there enjoying himself
and is rather indifferent to what is going on down here, or if one believes
in a God who can be bribed or propitiated by prayers or rituals – Plato thinks
atheism is preferable. This considerably narrows down the field. I think it is
probable that most of the people who believe strongly in God even in our
own day fall into one of these two Platonic categories. And so you can't
use *Plato* to argue that their brand of theism is more conducive to morality
than atheism.

CRANSTON: Nor do I wish to do so. But I think it is reasonable to say that
in our day, as also in Plato's, there is a considerable number of people whose
belief in a deity does not fall into either of those two categories. And I, like
Plato, would tend to maintain that the belief of this latter group is conducive
to morality.

TURNER: You don't give me any positive details about the belief of this latter group. Why don't you tell me, first of all, what kind of belief in what kind of God *you* consider to be conducive to morality?

CRANSTON: For one thing, I think it is obvious that a concept of a God who created human nature and intended man to reach fulfillment in accord with the laws of that nature, would be an inducement to morality.

TURNER: That might very well be so, if only we could establish the existence of a natural law. Then naturally, we might hope to fill in a lot of the details about the ins and outs of this natural law by getting to know more about the Supreme Lawgiver. But, as you know, we haven't been fantastically successful in turning up any such "natural law."

CRANSTON: You don't necessarily have to follow that order in your investigation. You could very well start with the belief in the existence of a Lawgiver, and this belief itself would provide the incentive to expend considerably more effort than we have expended in searching out the natural law, and to acknowledge its existence if and when we hit upon it.

TURNER: If you take that route, the big problem is to establish the existence of *any* being superior to man. You don't want to get into that massive problem of whether or not we can prove the existence of God, do you?

CRANSTON: I don't think that is necessary. Our focus here can be limited simply to the problem: what effect will the concept of such-and-such a God, e.g. God as a Supreme Lawgiver, have on morality?

TURNER: What *effect* ...? Are you becoming pragmatic? utilitarian?

CRANSTON: No. The pragmatist or utilitarian would tend to judge the morality of theistic beliefs or practices by the effects they produce. As far as I am concerned, it would be possible that such beliefs or practices might have what are generally considered to be "bad" effects, without the beliefs or practices themselves necessarily being "immoral." However, since the disbelief of many atheists and agnostics apparently centers on certain alleged ill effects of any belief in God on human behavior and moral fulfillment, my establishing the fact that it has good rather than bad effects might help to remove the main intellectual obstacles to belief, on the part of *those* atheists and agnostics; and could even amount indirectly to a kind of "proof" for the existence of God for those of them who do happen to think pragmatically in these matters. But in order to accomplish this, I must rebut the time-worn "moral" objection against theism that it is not conducive to morality. I contend that its effects are *thoroughly* moral.

TURNER: You seem to side with Voltaire – "If God doesn't exist, it behooves us to create one." (He obviously considered a belief in God to be necessary for bolstering the moral norms he stood for.)

CRANSTON: A statement like that could be taken two ways. It certainly has a pejorative connotation if it is used to justify enslaving men's minds with a specific conception of God just to assure conformity to some particular brand of morality. On the other hand, it might simply be a way of recognizing what I am trying to show here – that a belief in God, far from being detrimental to morality, is a boon to morality.

TURNER: I don't see how the idea of a "Divine Lawgiver" could enhance or enrich anybody's life. It turns me off. The only one who could possibly get solace out of a belief like that would be a "natural law" theorist. And the idea is dangerous, as well as unattractive. It could lead to conservatism in a very bad sense: "How can we change the laws that we and our ancestors have followed? They were laid down by God from the very beginning. He knows what is best for us." – That sort of thing. In sort, it's a cold and sterile idea, as far as I'm concerned.

CRANSTON: Of course. It's an abstraction. But the Judaeo-Christian idea goes far beyond that. It depicts a Lawgiver who is also a loving Father, who created man and is continually engaged in providing for man's physical and spiritual needs. That's hardly a "cold and sterile" idea, whether it's true or not.

TURNER: Is that the same God I'm familiar with – the one who is supposed to be perfect and supremely happy and unchangeable? I must say I have some difficulties with those suppositions. If God were perfect and finalized, as it were, it would seem that he couldn't profit or grow at all from our interaction with him. It would be such a one-sided relationship that we would have to conclude that nothing we could do would affect God in the least. The "loving Father" would be transformed into someone blessed with stoical indifference.

CRANSTON: This notion of an inaccessible and distant God seems to be at variance with the Jewish and Christian Scriptures, which portray God as intensely interested in human affairs, changing now and then in his attitudes towards men, and definitely affected by the actions and reactions of men. In my opinion, the discrepancy between the two notions of God is the fault of Christian philosophers, who have forced the form of an Aristotelian concept of the divinity onto a definitely unmalleable Christian content. I would opt for the more Scriptual conception of God.

TURNER: And this Scriptural God – would he be omniscient? It seems to me that even many non-Aristotelian theologians characterize him as knowing everything. And I don't recall anything from the Scriptures about any creature successfully hiding something from God, or really surprising him in any way.

CRANSTON: To a great extent, that's a matter of interpretation. It would cause great problems to me if God had to be conceived as completely omniscient. Knowledge of the future is especially problematical. If God knew everything we were going to do before we did it, this would seem to detract from man's power of free choice. I mean, if there were a kind of blueprint in God's mind charting out all of our actions with precision, I personally would feel that my freedom was compromised. If I couldn't produce something that would surprise even God now and then, my "freedom" would seem to be hardly more than a necessary chain of causes and effects. And thus I wouldn't want to emphasize an absolute omniscience on the part of God.

TURNER: Amen, brother, amen. And I don't suppose you would want to saddle God with omnipotence, in view of the fantastic amount of evil that the good God must want to stop, but apparently hasn't been able to stop?

CRANSTON: If man wants to perpetuate evil by his free actions or omissions, there is nothing God can do to stop *that*. Either omnipotence has its limitations, or "freedom" is an empty word. I personally think "omnipotence" has to be taken in a relative sense: God is just vastly more powerful than anything man can conceptualize.

TURNER: Do you see where you're going? You're developing a notion of God that may indeed be admirable and conducive to morality; but it does not even faintly resemble the usual and traditional idea of God that we are familiar with. And you know that the Christian theologians and metaphysicians would pounce on you and say that you've come up with a God that cuts a rather weak figure, indeed, and is probably even self-contradictory.

CRANSTON: So be it. I'm not afraid to take the consequences. Certainly this idea of God may contradict theirs, but it's about time they made the change. And so one may take our discussion also as a critique of some prevailing concepts about God, and a suggestion for revision. But you seem to think I'm starting something new, and I'm not. There are respected philosophers who argue for a finite God, a God with some limitations, a God subject to change for the better.[5] And I think there are many ordinary Christians who know Scriptures too well to be taken in by those other outmoded concepts of God. So it is with these "theological circles" that we must identify if we want to maintain that the idea of God has a beneficial effect on morality.

TURNER: Don't make any commitments for me, though ... By the way, I hate to bring this up, but there is this touchy matter of ... um, hell. Do you think this is going to be conducive ...

CRANSTON: I'm surprised that you should object to this. You seem willing to accept the fact that society enforces its objective morality by various positive and negative reinforcements, and here we have, quite simply, an eternal negative reinforcement.

TURNER: I rather think that our society in its more enlightened moods is a bit more circumspect and compassionate in meting out its punishments. It has an interest in rehabilitating offenders, and tries to avoid vengence for vengence's sake in cases in which the possibility of rehabilitation is remote. And, all in all, it uses for the most part more subtle and refined reinforcements, both positive and negative, than the threat of burning offenders alive physically and/or spiritually.

CRANSTON: Here again your overly sanguine view of the goodness of men seems to be getting in the way of a balanced perspective. And you seem to be taking for granted that God might be able to rehabilitate or "re-educate" those who don't particularly *like* him, which seems to militate against their freedom. Also, I think it is important likewise to emphasize that God as we conceive of Him employs and apparently does prefer the more subtle "re-inforcements," such as fatherly approval and disapproval.

TURNER: I am distrustful of this whole "father" analogy. Freud has turned up some pretty thought-provoking evidence that the idea of God-as-Father is an unconscious attempt of the human race to reinstate the tyrannical patriarch type who was murdered by our ancestors in various forms, long ago.[6] I don't follow Freud in everything he says, but it seems to me that here he may have put his finger on something. This idea of the fatherhood of God *is* a curious development.

CRANSTON: Even if that were true, I don't think it would necessarily invalidate the idea of God. Consider this example: There is a boy who thought he was an orphan, and was exposed to all kinds of tyrannical father-substitutes during his childhood. Then one day he discovers that he had been lost by his father as a baby; and that the father is still living and would like to reclaim him. Imagine the thoughts of the boy in the interlude, while he is waiting to meet his father for the first time. Since he has only been exposed to a rather negative type of "father," his concept of the father he is going to meet will necessarily be colored by his previous experience. He knows no other kind of father. It is only after the meeting that he will even begin to have a chance to dispel the notions he previously entertained about what a father is like.

TURNER: Well, then, unless God as our Father takes the pains to arrange for such a meeting, how can we dispel our misconceptions, or even recognize them as misconceptions? Why doesn't he reveal himself? Why does he want to hide? What purpose is served by this atmosphere of arcanity? He could at least provide a picture or reasonable facsimile, so we could get an idea of what he is like. Or doesn't his omnipotence extend that far?

CRANSTON: Perhaps a certain degree of personal or spiritual development is a prerequisite before God could be "seen" fully, even if he were to reveal himself. That's what the mystics say. For a believing Christian, however, God is at least partially revealed in the Scriptures. And the picture you get from the Scriptures is a far cry from Freud's "patriarch." Especially in the New Testament, the Father is depicted as a loving, concerned God, who is provident as far as possible for all of his creatures, depending on their capacities and receptivity.

TURNER: Perhaps *overly* provident for his "faithful" ones. I can't help thinking of Feuerbach's devastating criticism of the concept of God as a repository for all of our finer aspirations which are lying idle, and which we are too lazy to do anything about. By projecting them into a provident God-figure, we can admire an unreal echo of our own possible benevolence and productivity and creativity from afar, without feeling any responsibility to roll up our sleeves and develop some of those potentialities on our own.[7] We just feel so happy that God is so good, so generous, so merciful, etc. that we are distracted from the necessity of becoming generous and so forth, ourselves. Now, I don't doubt that this sort of "projection" may have been necessary in the infancy and childhood of the human race, when we did not yet have sufficient self-conciousness to realize our potentialities more directly, and could only deal with them in an alienated "projected" form, to use the psychoanalytic jargon. But now that we're adults, and no longer have to project our finer creative qualities onto outside "carriers," we should rid ourselves of these remnants of infantile theism. We have to fend for ourselves, now. We can no longer get away with saying, "God will provide," "God will understand," etc.

CRANSTON: Feuerbach's God is a "straw man." The God *he* was attacking does not represent what I consider to be the mainstream of Christian theistic thinking. As I have already indicated, I think a more Scriptural construal of the idea of God is called for. And for the life of me I can't see how the opposite extreme that Feuerbach opts for – man without God, completely alone in the universe, dependent absolutely on his own *limited* resources even if he does have the love of other equally limited human beings to buoy him up now and then[8] – is an idea especially conducive to human moral progress. It's an essentially bleak and pessimistic view, and pessimism has never been a very effective incentive to any kind of progress.

TURNER: A realistic viewpoint, judged from the perspective of exaggerated optimism, is bound to seem pessimistic.

CRANSTON: I would say that the Scriptural concept of God which I have proposed is a realistic idea – of God, and the sort of impetus he can give to human endeavors.

TURNER: So what do we have left with your "Scriptural" God? Let's examine the residue: It's rather a compromise between theistic belief of the more traditional sort and outright atheism. We are presented with a God vaguely but indisputably reminiscent of our father-images, demonstrating some definite concern for men without interfering too much in their affairs, and showing some expertise in using extremely subtle positive and negative reinforcements to keep things going. – Hardly a charismatic figure to identify with, you'll have to admit.

CRANSTON: For *modern* man, living in a pluralistic and relativistic universe, that notion is probably as inspirational as an abstract notion can be. But you're right. It is *too* abstract, needs to be supplemented with something more concrete. And for the Christian, this "something" is the belief in Jesus, the God-*man*. Here is a figure that has provided an indubitable incentive for the highest levels of moral behavior in our culture.

TURNER: You're making it extremely difficult to determine just what idea of God, if any, is operative as a positive moral force. For one thing, who on earth knows what the real historical Jesus was really like? Doesn't it make some difference to you whether the God-man functions as a myth or as a real historical personality?

CRANSTON: I would like to remind you that, for the purposes of our discussion, it would not make a great deal of difference one way or the other. All we are concerned with are the prospective effects of this or that notion of the deity, prescinding from the question of whether the deity exists. However, with regard to the existence of the historical Jesus,[9] I think you are overestimating the problems. In spite of all the abstruse debates of the Scripture scholars, we have a pretty good idea of what this Jesus was like – a man of humility, simplicity and extraordinary compassion who was interested in gathering the ordinary "little" people together and giving them a sense of community and common purpose – that's the basic idea that has come down to us, in spite of the additions and distortions that the idea has endured down through the centuries. We can safely dispense with all the miracles, the prophecies, the 40-day fasts, etc. .... They are unnecessary adjuncts to the true moral influence of Jesus.

TURNER: Can you also dispense with the Resurrection? If you do so, I can hardly see how you could have grounds for proposing Jesus as a *God*-man. A transitory mortal God, lasting only 33 years, is a bit much to swallow even for the most broad-minded theist.

CRANSTON: I have to admit that is a problem. I suppose that a belief in resurrection in *some* sense would be entailed, if one believed in the divinity of Jesus.

TURNER: I won't press you on that point. It's not necessary. Even without any of this supernatural paraphanalia, the figure of Jesus is hardly a suitable model for morality. You spoke about his "compassion," "simplicity," etc. Well and good. What you fail to mention is that (unless this is another one of those later "distortions") he is supposed to have preached universal love and been given over to absolute self-sacrifice. I submit that a life devoted to such lofty idealism, far from being as is usually thought, a model for us mortals, can be very discouraging, and a stimulus to a heightened sense of guilt, inadequacy and frustration on our part, if (as is likely) we cannot measure up to such standards. In fact, I've heard it said that the reason the interpreters of Jesus added all the supernaturalism (miracles, etc.) is to make it clear that the life of Jesus was so far elevated above our own that we could not reasonably be expected to do any more than admire it from afar. Certainly not *imitate* it.

CRANSTON: I'm sorry, but I don't find the ideas of universal brotherhood and self-sacrifice particularly discouraging or frustrating. I admit, however, that they go a few extra miles beyond utilitarianism. They are, to use your own terminology, definitely "maximal" standards. But they are in line with the basic sentiments of morality and altruism that motivate people from all shades and stripes of ethical persuasions.

TURNER: It is possible that, *if* they were formulated with moderation and common sense, they might be "in line" with our moral instincts, as you indicate. But in this case, they should not be taken as inspirations or stimulants or catalysts for morality. Rather, it is the other way around. We would be judging these maximal standards to be "moderate" and "sensible" by *our own* prevailing moral standards. We have to judge theological ideals by these standards. God is good because he conforms to our standards of morality, and Jesus is good for the same reason. If Jesus is taken by us as a model, the credit lies just as much with us as with the model. Don't you see? The morality – I mean, the moral judgement – comes first. The models that are chosen – divine or otherwise – must "follow suit."

CRANSTON: How would morality pass judgement on that which lies *beyond* it? A model like Jesus certainly goes beyond all the usual humdrum notions of morality.

TURNER: It goes beyond our *ordinary* morality. That's for sure. But we have different levels of morality, operating side by side and simultaneously. Certain groups with relatively maximal standards of morality may identify with a moral exemplar like Jesus, on the basis purely of their own peculiar moral standards.

CRANSTON: This is the first I've heard of a "multiple-level" morality. What happened to the good ol' dependable "public morality"?

TURNER: The "public morality" is the morality of the majority, which, of course, is not likely to be of the extremely "maximal" sort. The latter will very likely be the morality-of-choice of smaller groups, existing outside of, or (if you prefer) going "beyond," the public morality. Their level of morality will be, as it were, a "minority plank." And I think it is only a minority who are likely to hold up Jesus as their moral ideal. But the main point, which I hope you won't miss, is that *whoever* extolls Jesus as their moral ideal, is implicitly subjecting Jesus to their own moral criteria.

CRANSTON: I'm not surprised that you hold this, because you seem to be supposing that one must derive his values either *a)* from the public morality, which supplies the "objective" standards for morality; or *b)* from certain minority planks which, I presume, fall short of objectivity. But there is a third possibility. In a previous discussion you also allowed *c)* that, at least in an ideal society, an "exemplary individual" might be taken as the source for values.

TURNER: That would be the case of a meritocracy where the society happens to cluster and sustain itself around a nucleus of moral values, rather than the motivations of power, etc. that usually prevail. It's a limiting case, and, we both admitted, completely idealistic.

CRANSTON: Perhaps it's not that idealistic, after all. If we reapply the concept of the "exemplary individual" to religious societies as meritocratic subsocieties (or supra-societies?)[10] existing within the compass (or transcending the boundaries?) of larger societies, but existing on a "higher level," we have all the makings of an application that might turn out to be realistic, even according to your rigid standards. It is possible that some at least of the Christian religions could function in this way as subsocietal or suprasocietal meritocracies in which the exemplary ideal of Jesus would be the effective criterion for values rather than being subordinated to the moral value judgements of the group in question.

TURNER: In such a subsociety, it would be almost impossible to determine whether the source of morality was the society itself, which had managed to organize itself in such an impeccably meritocratic manner, or the figure of Jesus, taken as the model and inspiration for that society. At any rate, even in such a subsociety, Jesus could not be taken as an "exemplary individual," at least in the sense in which you introduced that notion previously. For if I understood you correctly, the "exemplary individual" would always be a *living* individual who would act as a moral pathfinder for society.

CRANSTON: I can see what you mean. But that is not an insuperable obstacle. I could say – and with good reason, I think – that the actual exemplars in the religious groups are those who keep the memory and spirit of Jesus alive in that society, and, incidentally, help to construct around themselves just the sort of meritocracy that Jesus instituted among his followers. I am thinking of individuals like Francis of Assisi, Albert Schweitzer, Martin Luther King. We might disagree as to which individuals should be singled out. But the point is that Jesus as God-man, even though no longer living, could still function as the ultimate determinant "exemplary individual" in those sub-societies or supra-societies in which actual living "exemplary individuals" functioned *vicariously* as his models and as perpetuators of the sort of meritocracy that would be necessary to give him the necessary influence.

TURNER: Since I don't have the faith that you apparently have, I'm experiencing great difficulty following you at the present juncture. Not only am I expected to perceive Francis of Assisi *et al.* as subjected directly to the influence of, and directly deriving their values from, a God-man who, to most of us at least, seems to be invisible and absent; but also I am to believe that members of meritocratic religious sub-societies would derive moral inspiration without becoming fanatics, on the one hand, and without succumbing to despair or apathy or negative reactions, on the other.

CRANSTON: I can do nothing to make the first hurdle easier for you, since that really is a problem of faith. However, in regard to the latter fears that you express, I would say that precisely this danger of the injection of fanaticism, etc. serves to emphasize for the thoughtful religious person the importance of a correct understanding and interpretation of the influence and significance of the central exemplar; and this correct interpretation and understanding seems to be precisely what organized religion is geared to fostering.

TURNER: Organized religion? Is this what you had in mind when you spoke about meritocratic sub-societies grouping themselves around Christ, Francis of Assisi, etc.?

CRANSTON: I would like to use that term "organized religion," in the broadest possible sense, to include not only the various religions which are usually recognized as such, but even looser organizations or movements which cluster around "Christ figures" and strive to perpetuate their moral influence. The main test that would be applied to such organizations is whether or not they are truly moral meritocracies – i.e. whether or not moral attractiveness becomes synonymous with power, at least within the confines of that institution.

TURNER: Using that criterion, you would have to eliminate all the religious organizations *I* am familiar with.

CRANSTON: But I think that some of these organizations approximate at least closer to the ideal of a meritocracy than is to be found anywhere in society at large, i.e. so called "secular" society.

TURNER: I'm afraid that we're never going to come to any agreement about this. What you prefer to call "interpretation" and "the correct understanding" of Jesus could just as well be construed as either watering down the influence of Jesus or using his influence as a justification for one's own moral predilections. Can you give me any solid evidence that Christian religious organizations (even in your "wider" sense of that word) have consistently or even frequently been at the *avant garde* of morality, i.e. going beyond morality just enough to offer moral direction and inspiration, leading morality but not rushing too far ahead into idiosyncratic extremes?

CRANSTON: I think the "universalism" of Christianity, which we touched on briefly in the previous discussion, is a case in point. I grant that the organized religions have very often been deficient in the practice of "universal love," but at least among Christian "organizations" in the looser sense the ideal of universal brotherhood has been fostered; and it seems obvious to me that this doctrine alone has had an important role in instigating the egalitarianism and cosmopolitanism which is the earmark of the more progressive areas of contemporary society. I also think that the doctrine that the "leader is the servant of his people" has had an important effect in liberalizing and gradually democratizing societies.

TURNER: It would be very hard to ferret out the specifically Christian influences responsible for such movements, and distinguish them from definitely "secular" influences.

CRANSTON: I don't think it would accomplish anything for us to get into a long analysis of history to try to ferret out the various species of influence. At any rate, I am beginning to see that the two of us, in discussing the possible moral "effects" of religious beliefs, are in disagreement about some religious "basics." You can't give serious consideration to the possibility that moral or supra-moral effects could be traced directly to the causal influence of God or religious ideals. You still prefer to see the latter as effects of environmental influences rather than as causes in their own right. I don't see how we can proceed any further, granted these presuppositions, or at least predilections.

TURNER: I have a suggestion: The main thing we're trying to get at, after all, is an understanding of the moral connotations (if there be any) of religious belief. Judging from our discussion up to now, I agree we're probably not going to be able to determine whether religious commitment (and we're speaking specifically about Christian commitment) has any special effects one way or the other on moral *behavior*. But that's a secondary problem, anyway. The primary problem is this: Does a Christian commitment (or any similar religious commitment) connote or imply any moral stand or *attitude* of any sort whatsoever? Does a person's religion *say* anything about his moral attitude? Forget about whether the moral or immoral attitude it fosters has the "effects" such an attitude might be calculated to have. I would like to know whether religion necessarily connotes any sort of moral enlightenment or amelioration of attitudes. For example, I think it is pretty clear that in ancient religions the religious rites, taboos, sacrifices, beliefs were only spasmodically and certainly *not* necessarily connected with prevailing moral values.

CRANSTON: Many of these primitive religions were not even theistic in our sense. There are also some very advanced and extant religions which are not theistic in the usual sense of the word – e.g. Confucianism, Buddhism,[11] and (in our own culture) some branches of the Unitarian church. But I think it is important for us to recall here that the subject of this discussion is not the relation of religion to morality, but the relation of *theism* to morality. We have gotten into a discussion of religion only because it seems that certain theistic beliefs may require religious organization for their perpetuation and proper interpretation. So we are concentrating on theistic religion, and specifically on Christianity.

TURNER: I won't quarrel with these "ground rules." Apply my question, if you will, to Christianity: Does a Christian religious commitment *entail* any moral attitude at all? It is not clear to me that it does.

CRANSTON: I think it does, and if you wanted to express more precisely what the attitude is that is entailed, it would be something along the lines that you yourself already adumbrated when you referred to Christian maxims as "maximal" regulations in comparison to other moral rules. Religion goes *beyond* morality; and the "maxim" of religion might be expressed as "you have a duty to go beyond morality," or something like that. I am willing, as you suggest, to put to one side questions about whether persons committed to Christianity actually *succeed* in "going beyond morality." All I am saying now is that, insofar as they take Jesus the God-man as an imitable maximal exemplar, they are necessarily also committed to "going beyond morality."

TURNER: And here, I guess, is the appropriate place for me to begin to bring in my thousand and one examples of Christian maxims which are calculated to bless and enshrine the most "minimal" standards of morality around and to place obstacles in the way of those who would like to go the "maximal" route ...

CRANSTON: In times and places in which religion has been allied with political and social power structures, there has no doubt been a lot of compromising, just for the sake of maintaining the alliance. But where there is some effective separation of Church and state, I think this sort of thing is less frequent. In fact a constant complaint about the Church is that it proposes a standard which is too high (i.e., in your terms, too "maximal").

TURNER: For example?

CRANSTON: Fof example, the stand which the Catholic Church recently took against artificial contraception.

TURNER: That's your example? Are you going to tell me that the command to breed like rabbits is a kind of "maximal norm" for behavior. I don't think we're on the same "wave length."

CRANSTON: I'm not recommending indiscriminate breeding. The Encyclical of Pope Paul VI on contraception did not prohibit birth control, but only artificial birth prevention.

TURNER: Fine, but the Encyclical did advocate the exclusive use of natural "rhythm" or "safe period" methods of birth control. And I don't have the foggiest notion of what you mean by pointing to these as "maximal" standards. In what sense do they "go beyond" morality at all? I seem to recall that the Pope himself insisted that the norms he was propagating were "minimal" moral obligations, incumbent on all men whether Christian or non-Christian.

CRANSTON: That was his mistake. He got involved too much in trying to sould like a moral leader rather than a religious leader. He was even appealing to "natural law" theories as justification of the norms he was setting. All of which obscured his essentially religious message.

TURNER: I don't seem to have caught that religious message.

CRANSTON: It comes toward the end of the Encyclical, where he points out that the unbridled use of artificial birth control, even in marriage, can be injurious to the spirit of Christian asceticism, can prevent the attainment of spiritual harmony and lead to egotistical self-seeking. *That's* what he was trying to get at throughout the whole Encyclical. If he would have showed a little restraint himself and avoided the moralizing about "natural-law" obligations, that's the message that would have come through loud and clear and, I think, the message would have elicited much greater respect, at least from religiously motivated persons. But the trouble with religious leaders is that they want to wear two hats, on the one hand making pronouncements about minimal universal moral obligations, and on the other exhorting people to supererogatory maximal religious ideals.

TURNER: Cranston, just try to calmly consider the implications of what you're saying now: That in the name of religious asceticism and anti-egoism, the impoverished parents of poor starving children in India should avoid using artificial contraceptives during the woman's "fertile period," even though that is the only time the man may be home from his work in a distant city, or even though the woman's menstrual periods happen to be hopelessly irregular, etc., etc. I use examples like this in the hope of impressing on you the sort of conclusions this line of thinking would lead up to.

CRANSTON: I am wondering why you should find this "line of thought" of mine so strange. I am, after all, following up on your own premonitions that morality should be independent of religion. For in asserting that religion essentially goes *beyond* morality, I am not only indicating a possible effect of religion upon morality, or indicating the (supra-) moral implications of certain religious commitments, but also giving an indication of just *how* the mutual independence of religion and morality might be *assured*.

I'm sure you realize that almost all of the great religions of the world have inculcated some form of sexual asceticism, either temporary or permanent, for the expressed purpose of facilitating the attainment of spiritual harmony and the loss of egoism.

Now, whether we're speaking about the ascetical pronouncements of Indian Swamis or of the Pope, these pronouncements are obviously not aimed primarily at impoverished traveling laborers or hapless hard-working wives with unpredictable menses, but at a class of people quite different – I mean the hedonists and materialists.

TURNER: Do you really think that a "card-carrying" hedonist or materialist is ever going to give serious attention to the prophets of religious asceticism?

CRANSTON: They might. But I'm not referring primarily to the out-and-out libertines or crass materialists. I have in mind those of us who are tempted in that general direction, and have the means to walk that tempting road if we so desire. If there is any purpose at all to religious asceticism, *this* is the class that needs the admonitions and exhortations. I admit, of course, that the Pope's ascetical statements would have made more sense if they had been directed more explicitly at this class. And what the Pope and other similar religious authorities are telling such people is: "forget about ordinary temperance and "decent" sensible moderation, which are the dictates of morality. Go beyond morality to complete control and towards the higher states of consciousness which emerge only in the concomitant presence of such control."

TURNER: Since you're using Catholicism as an example, don't you think it's just a little bit strange that most of the supererogatory lines of action recommended by the Roman Church, have to do with sex? Refrain from artificial contraception; don't add insult to injury after your sexual excesses by procuring an abortion; don't enter into any other sexual liasons if you regrettably have to divorce your lawful wife; don't artifically stimulate sexual passions by distributing or patronizing pornographic movies; and so forth. I think that captures the gist of the sum-total of the really explicit and definite official religious pronouncements made by the Catholic Church in the last few decades. I humbly suggest that the church should branch out a bit into other areas of morality – such as issues of war and peace and social justice. Why hasn't the Church said anything clear and definite and uncompromising about the use of atomic weapons, about racial discrimination, etc.? I recall a rather unequivocal condemnation of communism some years back, but this seems to have been elicited more by an opposition to the atheism of communists than to any apprehensions about the threats to social justice posed by communistic totalitarianism; and I notice that more recent pronouncements take a more moderate tack, as long as communism is willing to tolerate theism.

CRANSTON: First of all, Turner, I would like to remind you that at the outset of this discussion you were opting for the separation of religion from morals. It is hardly consistent for you to complain about religion meddling in matters of sexual morals, with one breath, and then go on to castigate religion for not getting into the moral arena, in the next breath. I think you exemplify the inconsistency of many people, who want support from religion when it comes to their favorite ethical nostrums, but a "hands off" policy when it is a question of sexual morals.

Secondly, even if I have to be insistent about this, I want to reemphasize that the conception of religion that I am proffering is a response to your own call for an explicitation of the essential moral connotations of religion, aside from the good or bad effects ensuing from these connotations. I have come up with a solution: that religion, freed from all the camouflage and claptrap, essentially connotes an orientation to "go beyond morality." This solution, as I have already indicated has the additional merit of showing a way to keep morality independent of religion and vice versa; morality being concerned with the relatively minimal regulations of human behavior, and religion being strictly confined to voluntary practices which go "above and beyond the call of duty," so to speak. Now whether we're talking about sexual morality, or the morality of war or discrimination, the place of religion is not to tell us what is right and wrong, but to make recommendations about how we can best attain a state of ideal individual and interpersonal harmony.

TURNER: In talking about all the "voluntary" practices inculcated by religion, you're talking as if all matters of obligation could be relegated to ethics, on the one hand; while all the supererogatory and extracurricular stuff would become the province of religion. But, in case you don't realize it, when religion says "such and such voluntary practices are recommended if you want to attain perfection or salvation," religion *means* "you'd better do this, or else you're going to rot in hell or purgatory or wander around as a ghost or undergo an endless chain of boring reincarnations." In other words, something *bad* will happen to you. A negative reinforcement is threatened. This is the language of duty and obligation, not the language of "supererogation."

CRANSTON: What can I say except that many religionists are going to have to work on their language, in the interests of greater consistency? What can you expect when religious organizations, which no longer have the "secular arm" of the state to back them up, are expected to utter commands and frame laws without any temporal, legal sanctions? It's natural that they should come up with a few eternal or spiritual "sanctions" of their own, just to "save face." But as I've already indicated – traditional practices aside – I don't think that placing a great emphasis on legalism and "other-worldly" penology is in consonance with the essential religious spirit.

I did want to add a third and final observation to the other two which I just mentioned, but I was temporarily sidetracked by your question about sanctions ... The third point was about that rather interesting emphasis on sexual behavior as a proper focal point for religious directives. Freud wanted, perhaps with good reason, to widen the notion of "sexuality" beyond its usual limited meaning and see it as a kind of key drive which controlled multiple areas of behavior and personal interaction which, offhand, don't seem to have any relationship to sexuality in the strict sense. Many Christian and non-Christian mystics have spoken in a similar vein. They seem to see individual sexual control as a kind of barometer by which the potential peaks of his religious aspirations can be gauged. Even the most liberal forms of Protestant Christianity are still bucking the worldly trend to saying, "anything is permitted in sex, as long as you don't hurt anyone." You can find the same sort of self-consciousness about sex running through most of the major religions down through the centuries. What's the reason for this? I suggest 1) that there is a kind of intuitive expectation (perhaps justified, perhaps not), that radical changes in one's sexual habits will cause correspondingly extreme changes in one's basic religious perspectives; and 2) that religious orientations may, indeed, as Freud said, be a sublimated form of sexuality (although the fact does not necessarily have to be interpreted in Freudian fashion as involving morbid repression).

TURNER: I'm sure that a devotional relationship to God *does* involve some form of sexual sublimation. But – and I'm going on my own intuitions here – there's got to be something morbid about this one-sided emphasis on sexual asceticism. It comes out just a bit too dramatically in religion.

CRANSTON: Perhaps we have been concentrating overmuch on the institutional Church. If one focuses more on the sort of groupings or movements that have developed around "saints" or charismatic religious leaders, it becomes more apparent that the true religious orientations go far beyond the sexual. In genuine religious movements and groupings, greed is at least for a considerable period transcended by simplicity and generosity; vindictiveness is transcended by forgiveness; abstemiousness and detachment outdistance one's gluttony and crass pleasure-seeking; and devotion to the common good makes idleness and apathy obsolescent. And all this happens not out of a sense of duty, not even out of a desire for "fulfillment," but out of a spontaneous redirecting of one's energy to nobler goals – such as the ultimate harmony and integrity of one's personality and the attainment of peace and unity in mankind as a whole. That's the sort of thing that I would characterize as "going beyond morality."

TURNER: I can think of some very weird religious organizations in the past and the present that have managed to mobilize energies in strange anti-social ways precisely for "noble" religious goals.

CRANSTON: Just as there are extreme moralists who give morality a bad name, there are religious extremists who work full-time at providing religion with its own bad name. But we mustn't take these extremes as our norm. That goes without saying.

TURNER: Perhaps, just perhaps – I think I'm beginning to see the thrust behind this whole line of thought – perhaps a sort of moderate participation in theistic religious movements or organizations (preferably of the non-institutional sort) is the way, the only way for a person who experiences what you called "Alienation $_{1\&2}$," to get out of it, by getting beyond it. You see what I mean? Religion as you describe it in its "essentials" is the perfect way for Kantian, neo-Kantian or disgruntled existentialist ethicists to escape from the self-perpetuating quandary of Alienation $_{1\&2}$. For those who have that experience, religion seems the ready-made solution. I mean, those who are depressed and alienated by their inability to determine their duties, and/or their inability to do their duty, and/or the very fact that they are caught up in the goal-making and choices connected with the alienated interpretation of duty – may quite understandably decide to throw off all this depression and alienation in one master stroke, by opting for a religious ideal which puts them essentially beyond the bounds of duty, relying on the intrinsic attractiveness of that ideal (for *them*) as a source of inspiration for maintaining themselves in a relatively constant way on a plateau completely above duty. (A religious person who gives up everything is not likely to be involved in soul-searchings about whether he should give up this or that; a religious person who is fully dedicated to his religious community is going to have fewer tugs-of-conscience about whether he has to do this or that for others; and so forth.) But for us "non-alienated" types, I'm afraid the religious "solution" which you outline is no solution at all. I, for one, could not get involved in the supererogatory works and life-style of even the most sensible charismatic religion or religious movement, without becoming, at the very least, neurotic. They seem abnormal, puritanical and/or escapist to me. But, for those whom they help ...

CRANSTON: You seem to be saying that man has a "duty" to immerse himself in this life and enjoy it to the fullest, without getting "hung-up" on anything that might involve real sacrifice or self-searching. It seems to me that the religion of many of your "non-alienated types" can be described along these same lines: They want to enshrine and hallow their pursuit of happiness (whether this consists in having multiple wives or caring for the body or the appreciation of nature or the satisfactions of philanthropy or just plain socializing) by making it into a religious "duty". So you see, not all religion is a response to alienated feelings.

TURNER: Well, if the alienated moralists need religious happiness to give them a respite from unmitigated duty, who can blame the non-alienated hedonists for trying to intensify their experiences of happiness by institutionalizing them and erecting them into religious duties? But as for me, I say with Shakespeare's Mercutio, "a plague on both your houses." I don't see how religion in either form is a necessary or even salubrious adjunct to human life.

CRANSTON: I think it is probably impossible to prove in an *a priori* fashion that religion transcends morality. Perhaps this is something that can be demonstrated only in one's experience. I would like you to reflect, however, that you may be doing *yourself* an injustice by rejecting so summarily the supra-moral possibilities of religion. You may, for instance, have fantastically advanced or sublime potentialities that can only be actuated and mobilized by the catalyst of a theistic religious ideal. The very fact that you are unwilling to take an ideal like Christ seriously may be a sign that you have your own fearful neurosis about cultivating some of the ultimate (supra-moral) talents that you are now dimly and subconsciously aware of.

CHAPTER VIII

ETHICS AND AESTHETICS

Surely the art of the painter and every other creative and constructive art are full of [graces and harmonies] – weaving, embroidery, architecture, and every kind of manufacture; also nature, animal and vegetable, – in all of them there is grace or the absence of grace. And ugliness and discord and inharmonious motion are nearly allied to ill words and ill nature, as grace and harmony are the twin sisters of goodness and virtue and bear their likeness ... Musical training is a more potent instrument [for the moral education of the young] than any other, because rhythm and harmony find their way into the inward places of the soul, ... He who has received this true education ... while he praises and rejoices over and receives into his soul the good, and becomes noble and good, will justly blame and hate the bad ... After music comes gymnastic, in which our youth are next to be trained ...

Plato, *Republic* III, 401–403

The task for art to accomplish is to make that feeling of brotherhood and love of one's neighbor now attained only by the best members of society, the customary feeling and instinct of all men ... Universal art, by uniting the most different people in one common feeling by destroying separation, will educate people to union ...

Leo Tolstoi, *What is Art?*

TURNER: If you're looking for something outside the realm of morality to bolster the cause of morality, I would put my money on aethetics rather than religion. Aesthetic experience is one of the greatest benefactors of morality the world has ever known; but, since aesthetics is not the sort to make impressive claims about its moral effects, these effects go largely unnoticed. The passages I've quoted above are rather rare exceptions to the concerted inattention to the "aesthetic connections" in the history of moral philosophy.

CRANSTON: I would question the "aesthetic" appropriateness of using that passage from Plato. For one thing, poetry is certainly an aesthetic form. And I can't help but notice that poetry is conspicuously absent among the arts that Plato would like the people of his state (the youth, especially) to be exposed for their moral betterment.

TURNER: Ah, yes, Plato did have a bit of a problem with poetry. However, it seems his problems were caused, to a great extent by religious hangups. He had a particular conception of the gods which poets like Homer didn't always share; and, like you, he figured the wrong theistic conceptions would bear fruit in faulty morals. (Music and gymnastic are much more neutral.) Without these specifically religious presuppositions, I expect that Plato would have been much more appreciative of poetry and poets.

CRANSTON: Just more tolerant, and even then not completely above censoring them. There is one thing you seem to be forgetting: Both Plato and Tolstoi believed in the rigid subordination of art to morality and religion. Anything which did not jibe with their ideas of moral rectitude or religious, purposiveness would be prohibited forthwith, if they had their way. Tolstoi following Plato's lead, inveighs against the writings of Sophocles and Aeschylus, Shakespeare's *King Lear*, Michelangelo's *The Last Judgement*, Beethoven's Ninth Symphony, and Wagner's Operas. He even went so far as to condemn the great novels which he himself had written while younger, *War and Peace* and *Anna Karenina*. Using his moral and religious criteria, he categorized these early works as "bad art." All of this draws the Platonic idealistic type of moralism to a fitting conclusion. I'm surprised that a thinking aesthete of your caliber would be willing to associate yourself with these trends.

TURNER: Very well. They went "off the deep end" and got into some awkward corners because of their ideological presuppositions, as many philosophers from many schools of thought have done. Unfortunately, they were both laboring under that "mystical" view of morality which you are not unfamiliar with, and they were prepossessed by the axiological[1] hierarchies which this view gives rise to. But at least they had the good sense to recognize the function of aesthetics as one of the greatest single factors contributing to an optimum state of ethical affairs in society. It is this insight that I would like to capitalize on and raise to the nth power. So many critics of Plato and especially of Tolstoi have gotten so wound up about the obvious fanaticisms you pointed out, that they miss the very important thrust of the argument of both thinkers – namely, that aesthetics is of the *utmost* importance to morality, and may even provide the key to perpetuating a morality that is perpetually optimum and healthy.

CRANSTON: Whatever be the merits of that insight, I don't know whether it is legitimate to lift it out of the context of religious and moral preconceptions that both authors apparently thought was natural and essential to *their* insight.

TURNER: Their own inconsistency gives us our justification for isolating the "aesthetical recommendation" from the religious and moral superstructures. For in both Plato and Tolstoi that aesthetical recommendation runs into contradiction with the severe religious or moral censoriousness. You can't maintain both that aesthetics is a great boost to morality *and* that only those aesthetic trends which are already in conformity with religion or morality will be permitted to have any influence. Clearly, the net result of a *thoroughly* censored aesthetics on morality would be nil. Either you must give rather free reign to the aesthetic or you must give up the idea that aesthetics can *add* anything in a positive and constructive way to the sum-total of what is considered to be the "morality" of a people.

CRANSTON: I detect a slight inconsistency of your own in these objections about morality dominating other spheres of human experience. The idea of "public morality," which you supported, certainly involved the use of a lot of sanctions, written and unwritten, severe and subtle – which gives it a "dominating" character, as least in my book.

TURNER: Whether it truly dominates or not depends on the social structures. In a totalitarian society, it is certain that the public morality would dominate. But not in a democracy, where the structures are expressly geared to allow for dissent, non-conformity and self-determination. Under such structures, aesthetic appreciation and aesthetic expression would simply amount to one important kind of "input" by which the people influence the society they live in.

CRANSTON: You think it is arbitrary to give morality or religion an a priori predominance over aesthetics, but aren't you yourself advocating a definite and arbitrary priority of aesthetics over the other spheres?

TURNER: If you are speaking of priority in the sense of "dominating," of course I do not advocate that type of priority. But priority can also have the connotation of conditioning. If something conditions or strongly predisposes me to think or act in a certain way, it has a certain kind of priority to the thoughts or actions which it helps elicit.

CRANSTON: I'm not sure what you're getting at. Are you advocating that we all become patrons of the arts, or join a "keep America beautiful" campaign?

TURNER: I would be in favor of both of those. But my interest in aesthetics in this case goes beyond art or the appreciation of sunsets. I am thinking of aesthetic "taste" in a more general sense, as an ability to respond adequately to beauty in whatever guise it may appear. I would include as aesthetic the appreciation of the opposite sex (in fact, to my mind, this is the paramount case in which the aesthetic sense comes into play). I would also include the cultivation of the social graces; the delights and "duties" of friendship, wit and the art of conversation; all the various crafts, from boat-building to cooking; all types of play, games and sports, whether organized or unorganized or disorganized; and even the very generalized ability to simply enjoy life.

CRANSTON: Are you sure you haven't left anything out?

TURNER: I admit that this is to utilize the word, "aesthetic," in an unusually wide sense. But I would like to point out that this is the etymological sense of the word: the Greek word, *aisthanesthai*, means "sensing" or "feeling" – an activity which obviously extends beyond the parameters of art and nature-appreciation.

CRANSTON: You do have to admit, however, that the term "beautiful" or "aesthetic" is ordinarily applied only to art, architecture, and/or nature (including the human body).

TURNER: That's true. Actually, there's a lot of disagreement even among professional aestheticians as to how far those terms can properly be extended and applied. But I side with the more liberal among them. If a football player makes a great forward pass, by God it's "beautiful" no matter what the purists says; if I have a really good conversation with someone, that's beautiful; if Chef Pierre puts together a fantastic *Gâteau de Crêpes a la Florentine*, it's beautiful even though it's just a transitory creation meant to be gobbled up by hungry organisms.

CRANSTON: All right. I think I understand how you are using the term. Now what has all this got to do with morality?

TURNER: My idea is that if we foster the aesthetic in all of its multiple and varied forms in society, many if not most of the so-called "moral" problems in our culture will disappear of their own accord. Preaching and inculcating morality may be the *worst* and most inefficient way of tackling "immorality." The indirect aesthetic approach may be the best way. I think it is. Give people good flicks on TV with a minimum of the commercial garbage, and good comedy without that grotesque canned laughter; foster sports of all sorts, even on an international level, and pump government money into recreational facilities for young and old (let's have some fun from our taxes, for a change); build large and beautiful parks right smack in the middle of our metropolitan areas; prohibit that chaotic intermingling and jangling of diverse forms of architecture and non-architecture, which sullies the skylines of our cities; clean up the air and the waters which surround us, and clear the landscapes of ugly billboards; clamp down on the weird combinations of chemicals and denatured "foodstuffs" that insult our organisms in the form of "junk food"; teach all forms of dancing and music and sports from the earliest grades in our schools, and give just as much or more time to these things as we do to the more "academic" stuff; promote romance among teenagers, widowers, divorcees, and even married couples – help them to find sexual and intellectual and personal fulfillment in their interactions with the opposite sex, and so forth. I feel sure that if we could organize the energies of people along these lines and sustain that energy, society would soon begin to wonder where all the crime and immorality went.

CRANSTON: Sounds like "bread and circuses," to me.

TURNER: "Bread and circuses" is a start. The Romans weren't all that dumb.

CRANSTON: Do you have any *proof* for this little hypothesis of yours? If so, you might be able to win some converts to aestheticism.

TURNER: I think I have a proof of sorts, although I'm not sure if *you* would accept it as proof. Have you ever seen those tables in which the crime statistics of the United States are compared with those of the various European and Scandinavian countries and Canada? It's a lesson in itself just to read the statistics. The United States is *monstrously* ahead in the *per capita* incidence of every form of violent or serious crime, from rape to armed robbery to murder.[2] The United States has over five times as much crime per capita as our nearest "competitor," Canada. And we consistently have every year 10–20 times as much violent crime as some of the low-crime countries, such as Denmark and Holland. Anyone who tells me that this isn't in great measure attributable to the great difference in life style in the U.S. and these other countries, just isn't facing up to the facts.

CRANSTON: That's a *very* subjective observation. I could accuse you of playing a very nice and presumably aesthetic game with statistics: You're leaving out what I would consider to be some very important variables, such as the relationship of poverty to crime ...

TURNER: "Aesthetics" is quite material and concrete. An aesthetic existence implies a certain minimal level of sustenance and material possessions.

CRANSTON: ... and also the high incidence of gun ownership in the U.S. ...

TURNER: The American fascination with guns from childhood onward is a kind of obscenity in its own right.

CRANSTON: Say, what kind of American are you? We've got a lot of beauty here, in spite of the urban blight and empty beer cans and industrial fumes and commercial cacophonies and crowded conditions. You can't seriously believe there is *so* much difference in the aesthetics here and elsewhere that it could give us a "handle" for explaining the difference in crime rates.

TURNER: I find it interesting that a little country like Holland, with more than ten times the population density found in the U.S., is almost slum-free, even in its most crowded cities, and manages to maintain pleasant and relatively pollution-free surroundings in spite of their very good and steady record in commercial and industrial progress.

CRANSTON: All I can conclude from this is that ... you had a very nice trip in Europe. *That* fact is really quite evident. But you have to be careful about leaping from idyllic musings about European vacation spots to asserting a correlation between the aesthetics and the ethics or crime of this or that country. Why don't you give up? I always thought I'd find a soft underbelly of sentimentalism in you, Turner, and I think this must be it. Or, to use another metaphor, could this topic be your Achilles' heel? Back to reality, Turner!

TURNER: After a command like that from such an authority on "reality," what choice do I have? I leave aside my European "musings" for now. But, since you seem to be a man of intuition, I would appeal to your basic intuitions here. Doesn't it seem almost self-evident that there is some tie-in between a deep and all-pervasive aesthetic satisfaction of a people and their ethical standards.

CRANSTON: This is neither more nor less self-evident to me than your utilitarian hypothesis that moral good is equated with the greatest happiness of the greatest number. In fact, your present plea for aesthetics seems to me to be simply a variation on that fundamental utilitarian "insight." In both cases, the "name of the game" is hedonism,[3] pure and simple. In fact, I wonder whether there is any important and discernible difference between the ethical hedonism which you have been championing and the aesthetical hedonism which is coming to the fore in your thinking now.

TURNER: In an ethical hedonism such as utilitarianism, there is an emphasis on the application of means to ends. Various actions are considered important insofar as they are conducive to the attainment of happiness in various forms. There is also a certain amount of calculation involved, since a utilitarian has to determine which forms of happiness are most satisfying and/or attainable, which means are most necessary or appropriate for attaining which types of happiness, etc., etc. Unfortunately, I think it would be possible even for a good bona fide and certified utilitarian to become so bent on these processes of *calculation* that he might lose or suffer a diminution in his capacity for *enjoyment*. What use is it to be an expert on happiness, if the acquisition and maintenance of this expertise so saps one's energy and strength that he has little time or capicity for enjoyment? For enjoyment is what utilitarianism is all about. Now this is where my "aesthetic hedonism" steps in, and supplies a supplement or counterbalance to such untoward tendencies in utilitarians (and, *a fortiori*, in non-utilitarians and non-hedonists). Aesthetic hedonism consists essentially and simply ... in the cultivation of the ability to enjoy present objects. It is not concerned with the adaptation of means-to-end at all. In fact, a real, consistent and functional aesthetic hedonist will manage to keep the utilitarian "end" (happiness) before himself most the time, and the *utilitarian* who does this will have the distinct advantage of knowing with a kind of intuitive clearness just *what* he is fighting or "calculating" about.

CRANSTON: I think I'm beginning to see what you're getting at. Your "aesthetic hedonism" is a sort of device for helping to keep professional practising utilitarians "in shape" and in touch with the ethical realities they consider important.

TURNER: You might characterize it in that way. The important thing about aesthetics is that it keeps this notion of "happiness" from becoming merely vague and abstract. You remember how Kant in a few places criticized the notion of happiness as being vague and indefinable? Utilitarians have a more sanguine view than Kant about happiness and the possibility of attaining it. But even for them, frequently enough, the idea becomes too vague to supply a viable and identifiable goal for activity. So here is where aesthetics enters, shows him what enjoyment is all about, surrounds him with concrete instances of happiness, offers him constant reminders of just what his goal is, and, in general, keeps him from degenerating into a stuffy and abstract ethical theoretician.

CRANSTON: What about those who don't subscribe to the utilitarian ethics? Are they going to be benefitted by your massive experiment in aesthetic programming?

TURNER: Of course. Neither Plato nor Tolstoi were utilitarians, but they quite rightly perceived the benefits that would accrue from aesthetics to their own conception of ethics. I expect that even a dedicated Kantian might profit from a steady inflow of happiness, although it might make him feel guilty now and then.

CRANSTON: You seem to be forgetting one important thing: All these non-utilitarian aestheticians you mention are definitely not "hedonists," even in their approach to aesthetics. For Plato, it was the spiritual form of a thing that was the prime contributor to its beauty;[4] Kant emphasized the subtle and subjective interplay of imagination, understanding and/or reason instigated by various sense stimuli;[5] and Tolstoi in the latter years of his life, of course, was unable to accept anything as beautiful unless it had "Christian" connotations or consequences.

TURNER: All we can conclude from this is that our hedonists themselves have been slow to realize their own considerable potentialities for effecting the outcome of morals, and that others, dimly aware of these possibilities, have stepped in to try to fill up the vacuum in their own way.

CRANSTON: A little while ago, you complained that Plato and Tolstoi advocated censorship and control over the aesthetic sphere, on the part of morality. You insisted that you yourself would not advocate this sort of moral control. But I can see no way that you could avoid it. If you're going to excise the ugly in favor of the beautiful, prohibit pollution in the name of wholesome living, tear down buildings to construct parks, etc., you will be exercising a definite censorship and control, which presumably will be influenced by your own conceptions of morality.

TURNER: There is a big difference between the rationale for the restrictions I would recommend, and the rationale of the prohibitions advocated by Tolstoi *et al. I* would disparage the ugly not because it is immoral, but because it is ugly. Aesthetics has an autonomy of its own: it doesn't need ethics to tell it what is ugly or beautiful. In judging aesthetic objects, one need not and should not bring in any extrinsic criteria, such as moral or legal norms.

CRANSTON: What would be the net difference in the results of an "aesthetic" rationale? I mean, what if the industrialists who are polluting the waters or the executives who conduct business in the center of the city, do not particularly agree with the aesthetic judgements of "society" about the necessity for antipollution devices or building demolition to make room for parks. I suppose society will just have to fine or imprison them in the name of art and beauty.

TURNER: Some laws may be formulated in the name of art and beauty, but their sanctions are imposed in the name of the *law*. But I think it should be stressed here that the laws in this case would be strictly "positive" laws, in the same category as the laws about driving on the right side of the street, not burning trash in unorthodox ways, not littering in public places and not picking the flowers in public parks. I mean, it should be made explicitly clear that there are *no* specifically moral grounds for these laws, they are just convenient instruments that society deems useful for promoting the public welfare.

CRANSTON: I have a hard time visualizing just how all these "strictly aesthetic" standards are to be formulated and applied to civic life. Presumably you're thinking of something quite extensive and well-organized. Are we to envision a board of artists, writers, musicians, architects, naturalists and all-around aesthetes dictating the tastes of the people?

TURNER: Dictating? My point is: such people already do guide the aesthetic judgements of society in a non-official capacity. They have an educative function in society, and they certainly do condition our tastes. Why not make a virtue out of necessity? Give them some prestige and power, and make their standard-setting official.

CRANSTON: An "aesthetocracy," you might call it?

TURNER: That's a cumbersome word, and would never catch on. But let's forget labels, and just begin to give the aestheticians free rein in our schools, city-planning and governmental agencies; let them serve as a clearing-house or sifter for all new and old projects or programs that could conceivably have important aesthetic ramifications.

CRANSTON: Would you like to see your band of aesthetes exercising control over religion, too?

TURNER: Why not religion? Can you seriously contemplate a strict aesthetically-oriented society which would permit pockets of resistance in the vicinity of every church, where maudlin hymns, grotesque art work and stilted rituals would be granted the "rights of sanctuary"? Resistance like this would seriously mar the total aesthetic possibilities of society. And who knows? Applying aesthetic criteria to religion might give religion a shot in the arm, and make it viable again. I might even start going to church.

CRANSTON: If only the preachers realized how easy it would be to get people like you within their doors! Just remove a few statues or paintings, hire some good musical talent, revise their rituals – and watch for the great revival to take place ... However, I do think you underestimate the sort of opposition your aesthetocracy would receive from morality as well as religion. Talk about utopian ideas!

TURNER: What's an aesthetocracy? Utopian? The only utopias I'm familiar with are the ones that never happen because they project some ideal which is too high for mortal man. But surely the development of the capacity of enjoying the present in all of its manifold aspects, and of enjoying the creation of a present that is worthy to be enjoyed – is not something too high for mortals.

CRANSTON: I wouldn't say that this sort of plan is "too high" for men. But I personally feel that if it were launched, it wouldn't have a chance of remaining afloat. Villains and antagonists would appear from every side, not only moralists and religious people but good old-fashioned immoralists. Your local Association of Friendly Neighborhood Pornographers, for example, is not going to be *too* happy if it comes into conflict with your little aesthetic censorship board, and the AFNP and its clients would almost be willing to declare war on society to preserve the basic human right of pornographing.

TURNER: O.K., pornography is a useful example. Now, the first and most important observation I would make about the notion of censoring pornography is that censorship has traditionally and perpetually been justified in the name of *morality*. Which is ridiculous. It's not immoral to portray immorality. But it may be ugly. And whether or not it is ugly is a decision for the aesthetician to make, on the basis of aesthetic (not moral) standards. It is utterly ridiculous for organizations like the Legion of Decency or the Organization for Decent Literature to make and propogate and try to enforce censorship decisions made on the basis of purely moral criteria.

CRANSTON: Those are rather extreme organizations. I think that many community-based censorship activities are oriented primarily towards preventing exposure of youth to pornographic things they're not ready for. In a case like this, the censorship is not in the name of morality, but in the name of social or psychosocial objectives. And that seems quite justifiable to me.

TURNER: There's a confusion of motivations here. No one, regardless of age, should be exposed to the shock and indignity of pornography. However, there may be certain works of art that are judged too mature for some younger people, because of social or psychosocial considerations. This is not a problem for aesthetics, but a problem for the public administrators whose function it is to coordinate aesthetics with other motivations in making practical decisions. But please note that, if these officials decide on age restrictions for access to more mature types of art, that is not censorship. Censorship from an aesthetic viewpoint deals only with pornography.

CRANSTON: I will restrict my question then to censorship in this "strict" sense: Granted that the censors show a consensus about some instance of pornography, what would society *do* about it. What sort of sanctions do you envisage? There's some very ugly stuff around that cries out for action – really raunchy X-rated movies, prurient and worthless novels, gross pulp magazines. You've already said that you think the recommendations of your board of aesthetic commissioners (or what-not) could or should be incorporated into positive law. If this is done, sanctions will have to be formulated and applied. How far would you want to go in incorporating these recommendations into "positive" and amoral anti-pornography laws, and then backing up these civil laws with appropriate sanctions?

TURNER: We would have to go slow. The very fact that society has done so little in the past to contribute to the aesthetic enjoyment of citizens leaves a lacuna which is presently being plugged up by pornography and the like. The answer is not to multiply laws and enforcement apparatus, but to *inundate* society with objects of beauty and reflections of good taste. Do this, and all these other obnoxious things will disappear of their own accord.

In the case of pornography the source of the problem is obviously *sexual –*

but what is not so obvious to many is that this "sexual" problem really belongs in the domain of aesthetics rather than ethics. What is society doing to promote the sexual fulfillment of its citizens? Society's function for the most part is a negative one – maintaining divorce courts, enforcing laws against sex crimes, etc.

CRANSTON: You want the state to set up dating bureaus of subsidize marriage brokers? Plato in his dialogue, *The Statesman*,[6] suggests something like this. I thought it was an interesting idea; but, of course, thoroughly impractical.

TURNER: Plato's matchmaking setup was devised primarily to further the interests of the state: and of course normal people aren't going to allow themselves to be regimented for the purpose of breeding some special hybrid of citizen that the state feels would best serve its interests. That sort of thing would be unconscionable in a democratic society. But – what's wrong with a little matchmaking and organized cupid-ity?

CRANSTON: You know that I'm not against love. Who could be? But just how far would you suggest the state go in contributing to the sexual and romantic fulfillment of its citizens? Would you, for instance, want society to furnish or license or support bordelos, "massage parlors," and similar rudimentary attempts at sexual fulfillment?

TURNER: "Rudimentary" is right. No, there's nothing aesthetic about that sort of thing. For various pragmatic reasons, the state might allow such "institutions" to function legally within certain limits. But the canons of aesthetics, if they have any first principle, state that there must be some harmonious interplay of complex factors for aesthetic experience in the strict sense. As applied to human sexual interactions, aesthetics pretty well rules out the superficial and impersonal types of sexual "interaction" as well as "one-night stands" and even well-organized orgies accompanied by wine and cheese or coffee and cake. The infinitely subtle complexities of human (and not just sexual) intercourse are lacking in such situations. This, by the way, is also the reason why the blatant emphasis on nakedness and the display of genitals in pornography is aesthetically objectionable.

CRANSTON: Would you have the state educate the citizenry against nudity?

TURNER: Not nudity, but nakedness. Full appreciation of the nude in art, photography and sculpture would be apt to make nakedness in pornography seem insipid and revolting.

CRANSTON: Would you "go European" and foster nudist colonies?

TURNER: No. There's a difference between nudity in the pleasant fiction of art and in real life. In art, there is an attempt to use the body to portray human character and spirit, or to "clothe" it richly with suitable contextual embellishments (in lieu of the usual type of clothing). But in real life, the nudist stands out like a sore thumb. Attention is drawn so much to the body that one forgets about the total person and the mind. As a preliminary to sexual play and sexual intercourse, of course, nudity is a very important stimulus; but intercourse itself becomes meaningful and aesthetically interesting only in the context of the *process* of multiple human activities, including (presumably) many fully-clothed activities.

All in all, nakedness is even a kind of symbol of everything that is unaesthetic, insofar as it is typical of the unaesthetic to be "naked," i.e. starkly out of context, or conspicuously impoverished in enhancements and embellishments. I don't want to get into the various theories of art,[7] but once again, it seems to me that the idea of a harmonious "organic" interplay of diverse complexities is central in every theory. And the exhibitionism involved in the display of genitals in nudism, definitely works against such harmony.

CRANSTON: The nudists say that for us to view this as "exhibitionism" is a result of social conditioning. They say card-carrying nudists in their colonies are not distracted at all, and find the whole thing quite natural and unembarrassing.

TURNER: I would like to know something about the high level of conversation and social and intellectual interaction found in nudist camps. I say that even from a sexual point of view (which is of paramount importance here), they are on the wrong track. The non-physical aspects are just as important or sometimes even more important than the physical, in fostering deep and satisfying sexual attraction. Overmuch emphasis on the body is too distracting.

CRANSTON: I'm afraid that a large block of potential aesthetes will have to undergo a rather strenuous program of re-education before arriving at the rather sophisticated appreciation of sex that *you* advocate. But – we'll try, Turner, we'll try ...

By the way, need I point out that the cases you have been concentrating on are chiefly sexual? You criticized me, in my apologia for religion, for concentrating so much on the sexual. Or rather, you criticized religion for having a bearing on morality which seemed to be chiefly sexual. But here you are also giving the impression that the moral "bearings" of aesthetics would be chiefly, if not exclusively sexual.

TURNER: I didn't mean to give that impression, but the sexual examples seemed to be the most clear-cut examples of aesthetic-moral interaction that I could use. I think this is perhaps because the fusion between aesthetics and ethics in sexual matters is more profound and significant than with any other moral matters. But there are other, non-sexual ramifications. For instance, I would insist that the fostering of international sports is an important "aesthetic" priority. Now here is an aesthetic move that I think could have enormous and far-reaching consequences on morality. Imagine, if you will, what would happen if the United States became involved in basketball and football competitions in which the Soviet Union was our chief rival. As the citizens of the two countries are preparing each year for the international finals, and yelling "kill those communist clowns" or "kill the capitalist imperialists!" – they'll little-by-little forget about killing in the literal sense. All the aggressions will be properly sublimated, and war will just gradually be relegated to oblivion.

CRANSTON: That's got to be the wackiest suggestion I've ever heard. Such international sporting rivalries might just as easily lead to World War III, as to a defusion of hostilities. Why don't you take that idea back to the drawing board and see if you can come up with something a little more cogent?

By the way, you must recall that when we were talking about religion and morality, you strongly objected to *my* trying to establish definite causal influences between religion and actual morality. And yet *you're* lapsing into the same thing yourself with examples that sound so far-fetched as to make me doubt the general principle that aesthetics is going to have a solutary effect on morals.

TURNER: You're quite right, there is a parallel between the situation in our present discussion, and that in the preceding one on religion. Rather than try to convince you of the general validity of the cause-effect relationship between aesthetics and morality, I will introduce a "transcendental turn"[8] at this point which is somewhat parallel to what you did in our previous discussion when you decided to confine yourself to the question about the essential *meaning* of religion as contrasted with morality. In a similar fashion we can here distinguish 1) the question of how various aesthetic influences might effect sexual and non-sexual morality, from 2) the question of how to avoid a "category mistake"[9] with regard to borderline issues in which ethical and aesthetic perspectives are easily confused – and we can confine ourselves to the latter question. Just as you had intimations about a causal influence between theistic religion and morality, I have my own intimations about a causal influence of aesthetics on morality. It is becoming clear that I will not be able to prove the latter influence to your satisfaction. There is, for example, just no way to show you clearly that massive international ping-pong tournaments with the Chinese will lead to amicable U.S.-Chinese relationships, or that universal interest in the U.S.

and the U.S.S.R. in watching televised basketball tourneys between the two countries will help defuse tensions. So, I will now retreat with composure and dignity to the (hopefully) less controversial thesis that aesthetic-ethical "category mistakes" are a problem and should be avoided and/or exposed. Perhaps one of the most appropriate examples to use is one which you referred to in our last discussion to corroborate your own version of the "category mistake" – the example of contraception. Many people who object to the use of contraceptive devices on "moral" or "religious" grounds may be really just expressing a basically aethetic reaction: the suspision that the necessity of preparing oneself for intercourse by the use of technical apparatus or pharmaceutics may detract from that spontaneity and total absorption which enhances the enjoyment of sexual intercourse.

CRANSTON: Many people would be willing to "trade off" *this* aesthetic loss for other losses that they consider equally unaesthetic – dirty diapers, crying infants, etc.

TURNER: True enough, but whether people oppose or favor birth control, it is important for them to *know* if and when their motivations are "ethical" or fundamentally *aesthetical*. I think the same sort of situation prevails in regard to many of the "perversions" – from homosexuality to masturbation to bestiality. The so-called "moral" reaction of people to these acts is really the result of their perusing in their imagination certain aspects or stages of the acts which are aesthetically repulsive. It would be educational and better all around for everyone, perverts and "normal" people alike, if they realized the strictly aesthetic grounds for the protests which such acts elicit.

And so, if we alert people to this sort of categorial confusion, they will not be prone to designate as "immoral" what is simply a matter of aesthetics. The net gain for society will be considerable. The "dockets will be cleared" of already superfluous pseudo-moral norms. Indirectly, this will benefit whatever remnants of "purely moral" matters that are left, by rendering them all the more conspicuous, and more conspicuously *moral*.

CRANSTON: I hope you realize what a very *subjective* norm you are coming up with. You speak about a natural "aesthetic" reaction to things like masturbation or homosexuality, but people have written books extolling the pleasures of autoeroticism and self-stimulation, and also of homosexuality. Something like homosexuality may be quite aesthetically pleasing to someone who has the requisite genes or hormonal balance, while masturbation may provide the peak of sexual experience to someone who is naturally "introverted," as contrasted with someone who is more socially oriented.

TURNER: Good. The important thing in my estimation is that those who oppose homosexuality or masturbation should know what their real reasons are for this opposition; and that those who favor such things should know what their real reasons are for favoring these practices, and not make a purely aesthetic stand into a moral crusade.

CRANSTON: You look upon the "category mistake" test as a way of avoiding disputes about causal connections, but I'm not so sure that the "category mistake" solution is any less "causal" in its connotations. By use of the criterion of the "category mistake," you hope to delimit the sphere which is relegated to "morality" and broaden the sphere of aesthetic *discourse* to include many things which are now often included in ethical discourse. That's an *effect* of sorts. Your "category mistake" is supposed to have a second-order effect on *language*. In addition, you certainly must hope that these second-order influences on language will, because of a supposed connection of language with action, also have some regular first-order effects on the way that people treat sex-offenders and pornographers, *et al.*

TURNER: Well, here again we run into the problem as to whether and how far metaethical considerations can be distinguished from ethical ones. I'm sure you must realize that this same observation would also apply to your analysis of religion and morality: You were talking towards the end about confining yourself to the question of what religion essentially "means," but you were certainly hoping that if people accepted your characterizations of religion as "going beyond morality," this acceptance might have all sorts of first-order effects on their attitudes towards certain practical issues, sexual or otherwise.

CRANSTON: If "confession is good for the soul," perhaps this moment of mutual confession is beneficial. Now that we are able to view the "category mistake" in a more realistic light, I would like to point out to you that the examples you have given of your version of the "category mistake" have been exclusively of the sexual sort. Do you think this is accidental?

TURNER: Yes, purely accidental. A perfect example of a non-sexual "category mistake" would be racial discrimination. It seems to me that here is a problem which is fundamentally aesthetic in nature, but is propped up incongruously by all sorts of irrelevant moral maxims, such as "one has a right and a duty to maintain the distinctive character of his own ethnic or community bonds," or "everyone has the right of free association." Here all the talk about "rights" and "duties" is superfluous and irrelevant. The basic fact is that people in general are more attracted to those of their own race. I remember once having a dinner conversation with a distinguished philosopher from South Africa. He summed up his view on integration with a sweeping reference to the unattractive formation of the mouth and nose among Negroids. *That's* what it came down to. He didn't want to take the chance of being surrounded by such "unaesthetic" types! Now, I will grant that there are many whites who do not find the appearance of blacks aesthetically repugnant, like this extremist. But I think it is a very common thing for whites to find blacks at least less aesthetically *interesting* than other whites, so that they would tend to set up hierarchies of racial classifications, corresponding to these aesthetic judgements. I think it is possible that blacks do the same thing to whites. For instance, blacks often have the same trouble remembering white faces as whites have remembering blacks. (The same observation would apply, *servatis servandis* to other races: we have trouble "identifying" aesthetically with the Chinese, Indians, Eskimos, etc. They just are not the source of as strong an interest as fellow whites.)

CRANSTON: Where on earth do you pick up all this stuff? I've never heard of any scientific studies on the attraction of whites for blacks or vice versa. You're making some empirical observations that are at best tenuous, and probably rash. One could just as easily maintain that an opposite skin color, or even opposite or different facial features, could be a cause for *attraction* if one is truly unprejudiced and open to aesthetic influences. I think it's pretty clear that the slave-owners in the old deep South used to be attracted strongly *enough* to the black women around then. Do I need to provide any proof for that?

TURNER: No. I have no reason to doubt that. But cases like this can easily be explained as phenomena in which raw sexual infatuation overcomes aesthetic indifference, especially where the white is lacking in aesthetic (person-oriented) sexual fulfillment himself. I mean, there was obviously not much in the way of personal interaction between blacks and whites permitted, or even desired, during that dark phase in our history.

CRANSTON: I don't see how racial discrimination serves as a useful example of the autonomy of aesthetic experience. In all of its forms, whether ancient or modern, it seems to be related to ethical judgements. When people have negative "aesthetic" experiences of other races, it is usually because they see that other race in terms of negative ethical values. For example, people who are prejudiced against blacks will often give as justification the "facts" that blacks are lazy, or irresponsible, or prone to crime, etc. Not many prejudiced people are as simple and amoral in their reactions as that white philosopher from South Africa whom you mentioned. If people *say* their racial judgements are based on ethical motivations, can we really play amateur psychoanalyst and claim they are mistaken as to their true motivations?

TURNER: Is it playing psychoanalyst to point out that those slave-owners who complained about the "laziness," "criminality," etc. of blacks were able to tolerate such qualities quite well in rich white plantation owners and industrialists. The same sort of "double standard" characterizes contemporary bigots.

It is vitally necessary that a racially mixed society should reeducate prejudiced people as to the real meaning and intent of the feelings of prejudice they express – that they are fundamentally just negative aesthetic experiences, which are *capable* of being altered or re-formed. You have to do something like this before they will submit to "exposing" themselves or their children to a wider gamut of inter-racial experiences.

CRANSTON: When you advocate education about the aesthetical "category mistake" as a preliminary to better social understandings and interaction, it becomes a means to an end. Now, need I remind you that towards the outset of this conversation you distinguished the ethical orientation from the aesthetic precisely on the basis of the fact that ethics involves this means-to-end orientation, while aesthetics does not?

TURNER: You're right. So I'll revise my maxim and put it into more scrupulously aesthetic terms: "Learn to recognize the true parameters of your aesthetic experience by avoiding the "category mistake." If you do this, no one will have to order you to begin to broaden those aesthetic parameters. You'll do it of your own accord, I'm sure. Try it, you'll like it!"

EPILOGUE

CRANSTON: In the previous dialogue you devoted considerable attention to aesthetics as a means for clarifying and specifying the notion of "happiness" which is central to utilitarianism but, you admitted, also amalgamous and unnecessarily vague. And I think I would have to admit that, if the aesthetocratic society you envision came to pass, utilitarianism as an approach to guiding ethical behavior would make a lot of sense, and even be *the* teleological theory of choice. But the plain fact is, most men are living in an admittedly non-aesthetic environment, where happiness is always "just around the corner" or situated in the future. In such an environment, utilitarianism is doomed to vagueness and obscurity, at least in its more general recommendations.

TURNER: Yes, that's a sad fact in an anti-aesthetic environment.

CRANSTON: Then I wonder why you would continue to hold forth utilitarianism as a viable theory in *our* extant environments. I mean, does it actually sum-up and epitomize the really important ethical orientations in various cultures, as you seem to think it does? The reason I ask this is that I have some serious doubts whether people are fundamentally oriented in even a "vague" way to "happiness" at all. It seems to me that the populace at large has its sights mostly trained on survival, mere survival or survival of the fittest. They talk about "happiness," of course, but *de facto* their idea of happiness is to a great extent restricted to survival-related activities – attaining and maintaining security, getting a sexual partner, keeping or restoring their health or mental equilibrium, building up institutions and customs which support their way of existence, and so forth.

TURNER: These survival-oriented activities are just one way of achieving or assuring happiness or satisfaction. Happiness is at least implicitly the goal of all such ethical activities. People want to survive not as if this were an end-in-itself, but for the satisfactions they expect to accrue to them upon their survival. But as people begin to formulate a more adequate concept of happiness, they are bound to arrive at explicit attention to what I have called the sphere of the aesthetic (in the wide sense) – which extends quite a ways beyond survival.

CRANSTON: But in view of the fact that happiness in the full sense is only "implicitly" in the awareness of most people, perhaps, in view of this present situation, the most practical and meaningful utilitarianism would be a utilitarianism of survival. I mean, if all societies, even democratic ones, are geared more to various forms of survival than to happiness in the "fullest" sense, then in terms of the approach which you yourself have advocated, you should be able to see the "handwriting on the wall": *a)* by descriptive ethics, show that the fundamental really prevailing objective of all societies (if you judge intentions on the basis of explicit behavior) is a particular species of happiness called "survival";[1] and *b)* develop a normative ethics oriented to evaluating various types of activity on the basis of whether or not they promote survival.

TURNER: The problem here would be step *a)* – most people would not want to say that survival is uppermost among their objectives; and an inspection of their behavior does not give us a clear and unambiguous proof that this is the case. I for one would have various doubts that survival is a primary objective for most people.

CRANSTON: Perhaps if a viable "theory" that survival is indeed the prime motive and rationale for people's activity could be put forward by psychology or psychosociology, descriptive ethics would receive the necessary clues and incentives for focusing on and sifting the facts relevant to its own corollary conclusions along that line.

TURNER: Perhaps. But in the meantime the idea that ethics should be concerned with the "survival of the greatest number" or "the survival of all as far as possible," or some such objective, could never be "in vogue." It is interesting, though, that there is a respectable *metaethical* school of thought which theorizes that the *meanings* of ethical discourse can best be interpreted in terms of "promoting survival." But the metaethicists who champion this theory, run into snags because, well, it is possible to ask meaningful questions about the rightness of *many* things that "promote human survival" – cannibals are promoting their survival by eating missionaries, Nazis were promoting their exclusive survival by killing Jews, many women getting abortions are promoting their survival in some sense by expelling fetuses, and anti-abortionists are supporting the survival of the human fetus by opposing abortion. You can use G. E. Moore's "open question" test[2] on many versions of this "survival" interpretation: If it is an "open question" whether some action promoting survival is morally *right*, then it is not metaethically valid to identify "promoting survival" with "morally right."

CRANSTON: What if we drop the verb, "promote," and interpret ethical norms as statements about what is *necessary* for survival? It would be much harder for the cannibals to claim that eating missionaries was absolutely necessary for their survival, or for the Nazis to maintain that killing Jews was necessary for their survival ... The metaethicist then would have to deal only with claims in which it was intuitively clear that moral rightness and survival were intimately related or even identical.

TURNER: And the anti-abortionists would have the edge in the metaethical sphere because it is definitely necessary for the survival of a fetus to leave it in the womb, whereas it is usually not necessary for the physical survival of the mother to have an abortion. I can see why you would have some tactical reasons for being sympathetic towards this approach.

CRANSTON: The main point is, this formulation of the "survival" theory would show some *prima facie* possibilities for offering a "naturalistic"[3] explanation of moral norms; and the theory might have a chance of standing as a viable metaethical translation of many or most major ethical statements. – Once validating the "universal" theory on the metaethical level, one might then feel free to make the "leap" to substituting the normative goal that is actually primary in men's intentions ("survival") for the goal that people habitually and ritualistically express allegiance to ("happiness"), thus avoiding many of the ineluctable obscurities or inconsistencies which are concomitant to the utilitarian formulation of the moral goal of an organized system of ethical agents.

TURNER: Cranston, even if I did come to espouse your modified version of the "survival" theory on a metaethical level, this would not necessitate or even justify my "leaping" to advocacy of the selfsame theory on the normative level. For example, a metaethicist might show that the ethical statements people make are reducible to "God commands this or that" – but this doesn't necessarily mean that our metaethicists can or should advocate taking God's commands as *the* ethical norm.

CRANSTON: It seems unrealistic to me to believe that there can be such a rigid separation between ethical language and moral norms and behavior. In particular, it seems obvious to me that if a metaethical theory about the meaning of ethical statements just happens to be corroborated by evidence (from descriptive ethics and psychosociology) that people act or hold beliefs corresponding to the "survival" orientation of their statements, then the metaethical theory will be incontrovertibly corroborated by these additional factual observations.

TURNER: I know this seems plausible, but it is important to appreciate the necessity of maintaining the scientific impartiality and neutrality of metaethics. Once the metaethicist starts including opinion polls or even professional psychosocial observations as a prelude to his analyses, or even worse,

tries to make his analyses jibe with a particular normative ethical persuasion—
he vitiates the objectivity of his endeavors. And in a way, the leap you're
advocating is a subtle way of jumping from an "is" to an "ought"[4] – which,
as you know, is forbidden.

CRANSTON: I can see how this would be the case with some metaethical
analyses, but in the present instance I'm not sure that the gap is as wide as
you think, or that the principle distinguishing the metaethical from the
normative sphere applies in all its rigor. I think that it is just possible that a
metaethical discovery of the sort I've outlined might be important as a
possible source for breakthroughs in normative ethics.

TURNER: I'm open to suggestions, but I hope you realize that I neither
a) accept the "survival" theory (even as you have modified it, in terms of
"necessary for survival" instead of "promoting survival") on the metaethical level, nor b) believe that the metaethical acceptance of the "survival"
theory would entail any congruent modifications of utilitarianism as a normative theory.

CRANSTON: I would like to develop three considerations which, taken all
together, might defuse these reservations of yours. The first two considerations
deal with your first reservation, while the third deals with your second reservation.

First of all, for an empirically-oriented person like yourself, I think it
would be obviously gratifying if you could come up with an interpretation
of ethical discourse which shows that ideas of "good" and "right" have a
basis in experience, individual and/or collective. (It must have pained G. E.
Moore considerably to have to conclude that our ideas of the good derive
from a kind of autonomous and unverifiable intuition, rather than from
exoteric and repeatable experiences of the actual world.) Secondly, one indubitable advantage of the "necessary-for-survival" theory is that it helps
explain the "ought" better than almost any other approach. You had some
difficulties with my supposition of the connection of the "ought" with morality, and were continually trying to water down what you referred to as
my "mystical" "ought" to a mere subdued "recommendation." But I have
continually felt that your interpretation simply missed the full force of the
"ought" as it is actually used (and not just by compulsive Kantians). Finally,
although I can certainly see your point about the difficulty and usually the
impossibility for making a transition from a metaethical to a normative
position, I rather expect that this is at least not *always* the case: I mean, there
may be some metaethical theories of such a nature that the transition is
permissable or even diagnostically "indicated." It seems to me that this
necessary-for-survival interpretation does admit of such a transition. For

example, it seems rather clear that the reason murder, theft, and incest are so universally frowned upon is that they are thought to be indubitable obstacles to the survival of society, and this sort of thinking just happens to be reflected in our language. It is not always the case that language parallels the actual belief that we would ascertain through descriptive ethics. But in this case, there does seem to be a parallel.

TURNER: 1) With regard to your remark about G. E. Moore: I don't think he suffered any great qualms of conscience about coming up with a quasi-Platonic ideal of the good in an empirically-oriented milieu. Ever since the time of Hume, there had been considerable doubt about the relation of values to facts, and Moore simply brought this scepticism (for which there was a very good basis) to its logical conclusion. I think we can take his idea of a nonnatural intuition of the good with a grain of salt. The important thing was his demonstration that the good was not factual, was not an empirical or existent property. 2) Now, the question is, does your observation about the "necessary-for-survival" theory throw any further light on whether moral good is a natural property or not. At first blush, the rather obvious connection of "oughtness" of prohibitions against murder, etc. with the necessity for survival, seems to indicate that perhaps we are indeed thinking of the actual fact of survival when we speak of "good" in a moral sense. But then, if you go a little further, and consider some other very strong "oughts" which people insist on – e.g. the obligation to honesty, the prohibitions against adultery – the necessary connection with survival becomes rather questionable.

CRANSTON: I'm not so sure. Could the human race survive, if it could not hope to obtain veridical information at all through the normal processes of communication? And what is the source of the laws against adultery? Didn't people think (and with good reason) that some stability in family relationships and natural defenses against veneral disease were necessary for the preservation of society? In many primitive and agricultural societies, wasn't the dependence of the husband on the complementary and willing partnership and labor of his wife a necessity for economic subsistence? If *we* do not consider non-adultery as important as our ancestors, the reason for this is probably that we do not see it as necessary for *our* survival.

TURNER: I'm sure that many people nowadays would be absolutely morally opposed to adultery or dishonesty, and their reasons for this would not be connected with ideas about survival.

CRANSTON: They would be subscribing to traditional ideas that were originally inspired by the survival motivation.

TURNER: Well, then, survival is not explicitly operative in the intentions of many people who actually subscribe to those ideas *now*.

CRANSTON: Those for whom "survival" is not the operative motivation may be primarily influenced by motivations that are not strictly ethical at all, for instance, religious or aesthetic motivations.

Let me ask you this: Do you doubt that there is some correlation between *a)* the intensity with which the necessary connection of this or that conduct with survival is felt, and *b)* the degree of "oughtness" or obligation which attaches to the corresponding moral command or prohibition? (In other words, if there are oughts which we are not willing to suffer for, or even get very excited about – doesn't this show that we do not consider them very important to our own survival and/or the survival of our species?)

TURNER: If you wanted to establish a hierarchy like that, then *suicide* would become the archexample of moral turpitude, since it shows the greatest scorn for the instinct of *self*-preservation, which seems to be the main consideration in a "survival" schema.

CRANSTON: Yes, but let's broaden that a bit: Suicide either of the individual or of the human species.

TURNER: Then – in both cases – your hierarchy doesn't seem to jibe with the facts. I don't think it is the case that people consider it worse for an individual to commit suicide than for him to murder someone else. Also, with respect to the "suicide" of the human race as a whole – with nuclear explosives we have now in our generation for the first time arrived at the point where it would be *possible* to commit mass suicide by a nuclear war – and I am not aware that this possibility, which almost all of us know about, is of the deepest or most intense moral concern to us.

CRANSTON: I don't think that either of these considerations is a conclusive counterexample: The important thing with regard to individual survival values is whether the individual *himself* thinks killing himself would be worse than murdering someone else. I think he would tend to make this judgement. Then again, with regard to the possibility of a nuclear holocaust – one has to make a distinction between long-range and short-range orientations to survival. The danger of such an eventuality seems more remote than other dangers, and one's judgement is affected by this.

TURNER: I would disagree with you on both counts: It goes without saying that there are individual suicides who have never murdered anyone, and would never even allow themselves to think of harming someone – but yet show no qualms of conscience about exterminating themselves. Also, how can you say that the possibility of nuclear extinction which could become a fact right *now* within a very few hours – is a "remote" possibility? You're wrong on the facts.

CRANSTON: Of course the main "facts" we should be concerned with here are the actual opinions and reactions of people – which is the subject of descriptive ethics.

TURNER: If descriptive ethics were to show me conclusively that people actually feel the way you think they do about suicide (individual or racial) I might as a result of this "test case" begin to think seriously about substituting your "survival" theory for utilitarianism on the normative level. But, in the meantime, I think it is obvious that people – at least people in our culture – are much more geared to happiness than to mere survival. Actually, it just occured to me that your kind suggestions for a modification of utilitarianism may show just a little tinge of self-seeking on your part (I wouldn't think of mentioning your "survival" as an ethicist): You've been looking unsuccessfully for an updated and viable "natural law" theory, and the "survival" idea might just happen to fit that bill.

CRANSTON: If through the findings of descriptive ethics you became convinced that, in spite of what people say or even think about their values, self-preservation or survival is at the top of their hierarchy of values – would this have an effect on you metaethically?

TURNER: Can descriptive ethics go so far – claiming people have certain values even though they neither think nor assert that they do have such values? I think not, unless we are to suppose that descriptive ethics has some sort of priviledged access to an "unconscious" level of attitudes and values. And I certainly could not make that supposition conscientiously.

Now, as regards (3) the metaethical ramifications of the "survival" theory, I think that if, due to information received from descriptive ethics and other sources, I were to become convinced that "happiness" as the human goal should be specified more precisely as "survival," and if in an entirely independent fashion I were to discover definite survival connotations predominating in ordinary discourse, I would be inclined to take the one as additional confirmation for the other. But I still cannot make a jump from the one to the other. The laws of discourse do not necessarily coincide with psychological laws or laws of behavior.

Now unless you have some further critical darts to throw my way, I would like to make some critical observations regarding your own theory, before clude these discussions.

CRANSTON: Please proceed; the floor is yours.

TURNER: I have a suggestion for you that might help to shape up and improve this theory. It has occured to me that there is a more-than-passing similarity between your view of the inner-becoming-outer as the "objective₂" criterion of morality *par excellence*, and Dewey's notion[5] that moral good consists in a harmonious and constructive interaction of the human organism with its environment (so that present incompatibilities get caught up and assimilated into the imaginative progress towards future goals). There's a dialectic in Dewey, who, like you, was at least an erstwhile student of Hegel. I think you should find that dialectic interesting, because of your well-known propensities. I also find it interesting, because it helps me to spell out what I find most unacceptable in your inner-outer idea: the one-sidedness of the whole thing. Why should inner ideals and aspirations have some kind of a privileged position in determining objective norms for morality? Dewey had due respect for environmental factors and he presents, it seems to me, a more balanced point of view. More specifically, I think that your own idea, duly counterbalanced with Dewey's insight, might offer a rather interesting version of "objective morality" that even I could live with, if not embrace wholeheartedly. I mean, instead of "objectivity" being either some external norm (which you objected to) or some purely internal ideal (which I objected to), it might consist, in one restricted sense, precisely in maintaining a dynamic ("dialectical," if you wish) equilibrium between the individual consciousness and its physical and social environment. "Objective morality," then would be any state of affairs in which the individual was in a nice state of interaction or even constructive opposition with his environment, and vice versa. How's that for a compromise offer that I'm sure you can't refuse?

CRANSTON: The idea is attractive, but not irresistable. In particular, I would take exception to the way you have managed to do away with universality in the name of "objectivity." Your concentration is all on the particular interactions that take place between each individual and his situational environment.

TURNER: There *is* a universality here, if you go beyond textbook definitions of "universality": *Every* individual in optimal equilibrium with *whatever* environment he encounters ...

CRANSTON: That statement bears the earmarks of formal universality; but when we arrived at working out the details of content, the universality would become just as ephemeral as is the case with practical applications of the Kantian categorical imperative. But even if we could generate some universality content-wise with this Deweyan formulation, I would still object to it: First of all, Dewey construes "environment" too arbitrarily for my taste. He is thinking primarily of practical problems and obstacles that present themselves in the working out of each person's own continuum of means-end-means-end, etc. But this is to unduly restrict the notion of the environment which is *morally* relevant. I should think that "environment" here would include the ideological "environment" that I either receive from traditional sources or have created from the inner recesses of my mind.

TURNER: That's not a fatal defect. William James, whose approach to morals is very similar to Dewey's, is willing to admit such a wider connotation for "environment." An amalgam of Dewey and James might provide the sort of modification you are looking for.

CRANSTON: Yes, provided I was willing to look (as James did) upon ideas and ideals as fluid and relative chains of impressions. But even if I *were* willing to do so, I perceive something more decidedly fatal in even such a "modified" theory: There is still that old emphasis on responding "effectively" to the external environment, and one's morality would be judged to a great extent on how successful he was in doing this. Now, we could interpret this as meaning, ideally, that one is "selective" in responding to environmental imperatives; but, practically speaking, it is often impossible to be properly selective. For example one who is born into an environment of pernicious Mafiosi and knows nothing else, could not be moral by adopting to it in *any* way. The only way objective morality could come on the scene would be through his resolute abandonment of his environment, instigated by conscience.

TURNER: I could come up with counter-examples in which one must abandon the dictates of a false and imperious conscience in order to adapt to the exigencies of his environment – but I know better than to pursue this any further. The only thing I would want to insist on here, is that your inner-outer type of moralist would have to take due account of the external factors in his environment. An analogy with the artist might help: any artist "worth his salt" will not content himself with imposing the abstract rules he has learned by rote or even the strong passional inspirations of the moment on his environment arbitrarily, but will devote much concentration and energy in adapting himself to the materials or situations or context he is dealing with, as well as his intended audience. So also the moral theorist, even in your sense, must avoid any imposition of formal ideas and must even take his "inspiration," so to speak, from the quite external and factual situations he is dealing with.

CRANSTON: I don't have any great and formidable objections to what you are saying, but I do have some reservations about the reasons for which I surmise you are suggesting what you are suggesting. Sure, we must take into account all the "externals." But when you suggest that this must be done, you seem to be supposing that, after all, if it were not for these externals, there would not be much there at all to supply the grist for our moral mills. In other words, you seem to think that there are not any really meaningful moral determinations or forms that could derive in a kind of autonomous way from the psyche itself. The moral consciousness for you is a kind of epiphenomenon of, or even excrescence on, the "really real" factual and material situations of moral significance.

TURNER: I think that's a rather extreme way of putting it. I think that empirical input is of the utmost importance for correct moral decision-making, but I don't look upon moral consciousness as an "excrescence" or anything like that.

On the other hand, it seems to me that the sort of "autonomous moral determinations" brought to bear upon external reality by our inner psychic volitions must be extremely vague and abstract sorts of entities. I'm not really sure what you might have in mind in referring to them.

CRANSTON: These inner determinations are necessarily general in their thrust, but not in any way vague or indefinite. In fact, I think I can enumerate the major determinations quite definitely: The first is *honesty*, that what we do extrinsically should really conform to our inner intentions and feelings, or that we should not resort to any form of dissimulation or hypocrisy or conformism in the moral positions we take. The second is *courage*, which connotes the willingness to bring our genuine moral insights out into the open, and not to keep them "hidden under a bushel" for fear of the misunderstanding, mockery or persecution we might expect to sustain from others. And the third I might best designate as *"interiority"* – the habit of reflectiveness and self-consciousness which enables us to lay hold on our real and perduring self, and not to confuse it with the passions and reactions of the moment that might happen to become so imperious that they are confused with the inner sentiments of our real self.

TURNER: I'm afraid you've lost me on that last one. By "real" self I suppose you mean the "really real" self, or what you earlier referred to as the ideal self.

CRANSTON: Well, yes. I think your confusion or disorientation results from the fact that, while you see the phenomenal, empirical self as the basic reality in comparison to which the inner self is a kind of epiphenomenon, I construe the potential or ideal self within as the basic reality grounding the appearance of the expressed, empirical, self.

TURNER: We should have employed a translator to help us at these junctures of misunderstanding.

CRANSTON: It is interesting that at this terminal point in the discussions, although we are not ready to issue any "joint communique," we have at least become aware of the fact that some of the problems we have are purely linguistic, and might be solved by adequate "translation." You mention my real (= ideal) self as a translation problem. In your own case, I can think of some similar hurdles. The one that stands out most in my mind is the problem of translating your notion of the "ought" into my own conceptual framework. You seem to have a concept of "moral obligation," but you don't seem to mean the same thing by that term as I do. This is no doubt the reason why you were not extremely enthusiastic about the bearing of the "instinct of survival" on our human judgements about the seriousness of moral obligations.

TURNER: Yes, there is no such thing as *the* "ought" or *the* "ideal self." And, if this discussion proves anything, it also shows that there is no such thing as "*the* good" or "*the* moral." But there are at least two goods, two moralities; perhaps more.

CRANSTON: Yes, *unless* there is some overarching good or morality, which simply breaks up into the individual's responsibility towards himself and society on the one hand, and, on the other, society's responsibility to take individual determinations into account in formulating what you have called "the public morality."

TURNER: Cranston, your committment to reconciling the ideal and the real gives testimony to your inner virtue and courage. However, that is not a synthesis but a two-pronged reformulation of your own basic commitment to an "inner" imperative as the source and guarantee of morality. My own feeling is that, on a very practical level it is perhaps best for the peace of world at large if "you" and "we" simply cultivate our differences quite self-consciously, without trying to force them into the mold of some excessively artificial "synthesis."

NOTES

(The following notes, and the Glossary which follows are largely introductory in nature, and thus added primarily for the use of students unfamiliar with basic facts and aspects of ethical theory as currently taught. Their secondary purpose is to provide cotations or explanations that cannot be effectively included within a dialogue format.)

I. *"Good and Evil"*

[1] See Glossary.

[2] See Glossary.

[3] See Glossary.

[4] Plotinus (205–270) expounded a philosophy characterized by a hierarchically ordered universe descending gradually from the One (the eternal source of all being) to more and more inferior grades of creation. Augustine (354–430) and other Christian thinkers have utilized a quasi-Plotinian schema in explaining the existence of evil in the world. According to them, evil does not really *exist*, but results from a creature's failure to participate in the goodness of God according to its fullest capacities.

[5] I.e., an abstract and ideal universal Good, as contrasted with a concrete and sensuously immanent good is "Platonic." See "Plato" in Glossary.

[6] The English social reformer and philosopher, Jeremy Bentham (1748–1832), is a founder of the utilitarian school of ethics (see Glossary). He identified "good" with pleasure in its manifold forms; and tried to develop a "hedonistic" calculus by means of which the amount of goodness (i.e. pleasure) accruing to various actions, could be determined with some precision.

[7] The "thing-in-itself," as Kant (see Glossary) used this expression, is contrasted with the "thing-as-it-appears-to-us." The idea of a thing -in-itself involves the conceptualization of something "behind the scenes" which is taken to be a kind of cause of the phenomena we see, although not a "cause" in the strict sense (a cause in the strict sense would have to itself be something phenomenal).

[8] "Subjectivism" is an attitude in philosophy which places primary emphasis on the operations of the human mind or the reactions of human feeling in knowing, or even constituting, what are called "real" objects or qualities or situations or events.

[9] These "secondary qualities," which are produced by human consciousness, are contrasted by Locke (1632–1704) with the "primary qualities" (extension, motion, rest, shape, etc.), which seem to exist *in* external objects regardless of whether we perceive them or not.

[10] According to Heisenberg's "Indeterminacy Principle," discovered in 1927, it is impossible to have exact knowledge of both velocity and position in space, simultaneously. This principle applies to all physical bodies, but becomes most significant in microphysics, in which the difficulty of combining knowledge of position and velocity becomes most pronounced. In any attempt to measure the exact velocity of a subatomic particle, our very attempts to measure and the instruments we use will displace the particle from its position, so that this position is relatively unmeasurable at the time the velocity is being measured. On the other hand, if the scientist with his instruments gets into the vicinity

of a particle to measure its *position*, the wave undulations associated with that particle become so intense that they become relatively unmeasurable; and since the velocity of a particle is determined by a measurement of its waves, the velocity also becomes relatively unmeasurable. Ernst Cassirer in *Determinism and Indeterminism in Modern Physics* (O. Benfey, tr., 1956) discusses the implications of the Indeterminancy Principle for the philosophical problem of distinguishing "objective" facts from "subjective perceptions."

II. *"Is and Ought"*

[1] Scottish philosopher, 1711–1776.

[2] See Glossary.

[3] See Glossary.

[4] According to Hume, inductive arguments (see Glossary) are weaker than deductive inferences (see Glossary) because of their inability to substantiate any "necessary connections." For example, in the inductive generalizations we make about causes and effects, we tend to say that "A causes B" because of our habit of associating B with A, but in actual fact we have never witnessed any necessary connection between A and B. In interpreting Hume's position on the "ought," Cranston argues that Hume might consistently hold that our "oughts" are inductive generalizations about the fundamental (factual) positive and negative feelings or sentiments that people-in-general actually *have* regarding certain actions, modes of behavior, attitudes towards life, etc. Turner objects that such inductive generalizations, based on psychological evidence, would not amount to *derivations* of "ought" from "is," in the strict Humean sense, since Hume would only admit that *deductions* were proper derivations.

[5] Inductive generalizations are said to have a greater degree of probability when the appropriate variables to be considered have been isolated more effectively from other variables, when a relatively larger number of counterexplanations for witnessed phenomena have been eliminated, when a relatively representative statistical sampling of the factual data has been conducted, etc.

[6] Cranston in his earlier statement had emphasized the importance of eliminating obfuscating factors in trying to isolate the "pure" psychological variables, e.g. a feeling of repugnance for homicide, from which our "oughts" might be derived. This original position might seem to imply that opposing tendencies, e.g. a certain attraction for homicide conflicting with one's basic repugnance, would also be considered "obfuscating" factors, and would also have to be eliminated. Cranston here admits that this would not be necessary or desirable, since a certain amount of conflict in our sentiments is necessary if they are to give rise to an "ought" in the strict sense.

[7] The "ideal self" is a blanket term that might be loosely applied to such wide-ranging notions as Kant's "transcendental ego," Kierkegaard's "ideal self," Freud's "superego," and the behavioral psychologists' "level of aspiration." At its bare minimum, it connotes some notion or aspect of the self which goes beyond the present factual state as a higher state, whether attainable or unattainable. Cranston tends to interpret the ideal self as a *potentiality* for higher or better future states and attainments, actually existing along with the actual or factual self one experiences in the present.

[8] Kierkegaard (1813–1855) distinguished three spheres of existence in life, ranging from lowest to highest: in the "aesthetic sphere," one is primarily concerned with immediate gratification, although very sophisticated and complicated stratagems may be required to maintain gratifications at an optimum level and pitch; in the "ethical sphere" the individual reaches out for the universal as manifested to him through his own consciousness of his higher potentialities; and in the "religious sphere" the individual goes even beyond the universal to a personal Absolute, i.e. a direct relationship to God through faith.

[9] "The ideal" is described here as involving the desire to overcome any kind of Aliena-

tion, even amoral. It is important to say this, because otherwise this ideal, which is taken by Cranston to be the source of the moral point of view, might be defined as the desire to transcend specifically *moral* alienation, which would give rise to the circular question "how then does alenation become moral?" It is improbable that a really trivial or superficial species of alienation could be the instigating source for this ideal. In any case the "intention" of the person who conceives this ideal would render even superficial Alienations$_1$ more serious and morally relevant then they seemed to be. Cranston is arguing to the effect that it is the very consciousness of the importance of transcending *all* intrapsychic conflicts that puts an individual on the level of what is called "morality."

[10] See Glossary.

[11] See Glossary.

III. *"Virtue and Temperament"*

[1] According to Plato, the soul, which during life is confined in a material body but is essentially independent of matter, is perfected by four virtues – temperance, courage, prudence and justice. Aristotle modified the Platonic notion of the independence of the soul, allowing that the soul might be "independent" of the body only in certain specified intellectual operations; and spoke of "virtues" as the variety of "habits" which a person can inculcate in his soul by repetition of the best types of rational activity (see "Aristotle" in Glossary).

[2] "Faculty psychology," no longer in vogue, used to maintain that the mind consisted of various distinct faculties – e.g. mind, will, memory, imagination, feeling – each of which functioned independently of the other and (according to some authors) might even be located in concomitance to this or that bodily organ.

[3] The ancient theory of the four temperaments hypothesized that there were four basic temperament types which influenced human behavior: namely, melancholic, choleric, phlegmatic and sanguine. These four types were supposed to be caused, respectively, by a predominance of black bile, yellow bile, phlegm and blood in the body. Nineteenth-century German psychologists tried to update the physical aspects of the theory in terms of modern physiological knowledge. The theory has been largely superseded by others now, although one still occasionally finds attempts to validate the strictly psychological tetradic dimensions of the theory.

[4] The German psychiatrist, Ernst Kretschmer (1888–1964), hypothesized a relationship between schizophrenia and an asthenic or leptosome (thin, delicate) body-type, which tended to be introverted; and between manic-depressive psychosis and the short, thick, rotund and extroverted "pyknic" type. Intermediate between these two types were the "athletic" and "dysplastic" types.

[5] The best-known American theory of temperament-and-body-types has been developed by the psychologist and physician, William Sheldon of Harvard. The easy-going and outgoing "viscerotonic" temperament is said by Sheldon to correlate positively with the often obese and rounded endomorphic body-type; the athletic, energetic and extroverted "somatotonic" temperament with the muscular and erect physique of the "mesomorphic" body-type; and the introverted and often inhibited "cerebrotonic" temperament with a thin and muscularly deficient physique. Sheldon's methods differ from previous methods in emphasizing the use of statistical ratings and factoring techniques, and in interpreting "types" in terms of clusters of specific components.

[6] A masochist is one who derives pleasure, sometimes sexual pleasure, from being hurt, tortured or humiliated.

[7] In psychological parlance, "sublimation" is the directing of raw instinctual drives into socially acceptable channels, e.g. the sublimation of sexual impulses in marriage and family life, or the sublimation of aggressive impulses in sporting competitions. Some

philosophers, particularly Nietzsche, have used the term in a somewhat different way, deemphasizing "social acceptability": for example, when Nietzsche speaks of "sublimated sexuality," he does not have in mind adaptation to social expectations but sexuality's convergence with, and intensification of, higher and creative spiritual impulses.

[8] See Glossary.

[9] "Ockham's razor," or the "Law of Parsimony," states that "entities should not be multiplied unnecessarily." As applied to philosophy, the meaning is that the simplest possible explanatory principles should always be used, and superfluous considerations eschewed.

[10] See Glossary.

[11] See Glossary.

[12] The notion of "free will" in philosophy sometimes is taken to mean that there is some segment of human personality which is impervious to determination by physical necessities or environmental conditions; in other words, that man by means of free will is able to transcend merely physical determinants. For some, this implies that free will itself is a power or faculty existing in its own right in the "metaphysical" order, e.g. as a potentiality of an immaterial soul.

[13] Thomas Hobbes (1588–1679) was a British empiricist famous in social philosophy for this theory of the emergence of the political state as a solution to the fear and chaos caused by the conflict of the raw impulses of pre-political men in the "state of nature." "Liberty," in the Hobbesian context, does not imply any special ability or faculty in man to escape circumstantial determination; but only the creation by men of a social situation which would allow the greatest possible amount of unrestricted activity and personal satisfaction. For Hobbes, such a situation necessarily implied the existence of a strong sovereign (monarch) who would oversee and guarantee such liberty among his subjects.

IV. "Subjective and Objective Morality"

[1] See p. 128, n. 8.

[2] See Glossary.

[3] See above, p. 34

[4] See Glossary.

[5] See Glossary.

[6] See Glossary.

[7] In ethics a first-order consideration is concerned with judgements about right and wrong, while a second-order consideration would be concerned with judgements *about* these ethical *judgements.*

[8] See "Intuitionism" in Glossary.

[9] See Glossary.

[10] Matthew, VII.

[11] The German philosopher, Friedrich Nietzsche (1844–1900), was opposed to mass movements, democracy and all forms of egalitarianism; and proposed, as an antidote to such trends, the ideal of the Superman, the man who surpasses not only others but even himself in attaining affirmative and creative individuality and a kind of divinity (Nietzsche was an atheist). Some of these Supermen would be concerned with political leadership, and these individuals would have the capacity for imposing their own aristocratic standards on the masses with a minimum of force. Nietzsche's thought was utilized by German socialist ideologists as one of the theoretical supports for Naziism; but this use was unfair and unwarranted, in view of the fact that Nietzsche himself was clearly opposed both to the glorification of military force and to anti-Semitism. For a dialogic analysis of the Nietzschean value schema, see *The Unbinding of Prometheus: Towards a Philosophy of Revolution*, by H.P. Kainz (Long Island, N.Y., Libra, 1976), Ch. III (C).

¹² *Op. cit.*, II, 4, 1105b; X, 5, 1176a.

¹³ Plato (see Glossary) hypothesized that the ultimate solution to the world's social problems could come only when those dedicated to philosophy became political leaders or political leaders were illuminated by a life immersed in philosophy. This would be the "perfect" synthesis, because such leaders, the "philosopher kings," would be lacking neither the power to implement their visions (something philosophers typically lack) nor a broad, all-encompassing worldview with a moral integrity to match (something Plato thought political leaders to lack, but philosophers to possess).

¹⁴ *Thus Spake Zarathustra*, Ch. 63.

V. *"Ethics and Politics"*

¹ See Glossary.

² See Glossary.

³ "Social ethics," as compared with individual morality, is concerned primarily with man's rights and duties in relationship to others, rather than the private moral ideals derived from an individual's consciousness of his potentialities, his purpose in life, etc.

⁴ Hegel spoke of the "Absolute Idea" as a massive cosmic synthesis of subjective and objective oppositions. This synthesis was used as a kind of schema for interpreting nature and human events both on the individual level and on a world-historical scale. Empirically- and materialistically-oriented philosophers often interpret Hegel as maintaining that sensuous, material reality emerges out of, or is created by, some divine Absolute Idea. But this seems an unwarranted distortion of Hegel's standpoint. For a discussion of the basic Hegelian standpoint, see *Hegel's Phenomenology, Part I: Analysis and Commentary* by H.P. Kainz (Alabama: University of Alabama Press, 1976), Ch. V.

⁵ See above, Ch. I, n. 8.

⁶ Democracy in its classical form is best exemplified by some brief episodes of direct rule by the people in ancient Athens, in which not only the choice of political leaders, but also legal and constitutional questions and policy decisions were decided by the vote of citizens in popular assemblies.

⁷ As many have point out, the basic moral rationale for the judgements meted out in the Nuremberg trials after World War II seem to have been that there are certain moral standards that supersede the public morality and laws of any individual country; this supposition seems to have been especially exemplified in the Nuremberg judgements concerning "crimes against humanity."

⁸ See Plato's *Republic*, (Jowett tr.), Bk. II (368): *Socrates:* "Seeing ... that we are no great wits, I think we had better adopt a method in examining justice in the state which I may illustrate thus: suppose that a shortsighted person has been asked by some one to read small letters from a distance; and it occurred to some one else that they might be found in another place which was larger and in which the letters were larger – if they were the same and he could read the larger letters first, and then proceed to the lesser – this would have been thought a rare piece of good fortune." *Adeimantus:* "Very true; but how does the illustration apply to our enquiry?" *Socrates:* "I will tell you: justice, which is the subject of our enquiry, is, as you know, sometimes spoken of as the virtue of an individual, and sometimes as the virtue of a State." *Adeimantus:* "True." *Socrates:* "And is not a State larger than an individual?" *Adeimantus:* "It is." *Socrates:* "Then in the larger the quantity of justice is likely to be larger and more discernible. I propose therefore, that we enquire into the nature of justice and injustice, first as they appear in the State, and secondly in the individual, proceeding from the greater to the lesser and comparing them."

⁹ I.e., a hypothetical premise. See "Deduction" in Glossary.

VI. *"Legality and Morality"*

[1] See Ch. III, n. 13.

[2] After the government-commissioned Wolfenden Report, recommending removal of private homosexual liasons from the category of "crimes" in England, was published in England in 1957, jurist Patrick Devlin's "The Enforcement of Morals" and other writings became famous as a restatement of the previous tradition that certain private moral offenses can and should come under the jurisdiction of the laws. Some of the arguments used by Devlin are similar to arguments preferred by Sir James Fitzjames Stephen against J.S. Mill in *Liberty, Equality, Fraternity* (London, 1873).

[3] Conducted by Dr. M. Sidney Margolese, a Los Angeles endocrinologist, Dr. Oscar Janiger, a psychiatrist at U.C.L.A. and Dr. Richard Green of U.C.L.A. (See *Hormones and Behavior* 1:151, 1970 and *British Medical Journal* 3:207, 1973.) For a similar study on females by Gartrell *et al.*, see *American Journal of Psychiatry*, Vol. 134, No. 10.

[4] The *"ad verecundiam"* fallacy in logic is ordinarily an attempt to gain acceptance for one's arguments by appealing to the authority of great men; in a negative sense, the same fallacy is involved when one points out that this opponent's arguments are similar to those asserted by some "authority" whom it is known that this opponent does *not* want to identify himself with.

[5] I.e., a citizen subject to the protection of the laws.

[6] Under both British and American systems of law, special courts of equity were formerly provided to supplement courts of common law, but in both England and America now the concept of "equity" has been incorporated into ordinary judicial procedures, without any special provision being made for separate hearings for disputes concerning matters of equity.

[7] "Conservatism" in a very general sense implies a tendency to preserve some situation, e.g. a social situation, in the *status quo*. The argument between Cranston and Turner here concerns whether an outer-oriented or an inner-directed view of morality is more likely to foster an attitude of conservatism.

VII. *"Atheism and Ethics"*

[1] Socrates was an atheist or agnostic in the sense that he showed no interest in the gods that were revered or accepted by his culture; but a theist, insofar as he expressed lifelong devotion to a mysterious divine "voice" that he apparently heard quite clearly within his consciousness.

[2] Turner characterized Devlin's views on legality and morality as a "conservative reaction." See p. 65 above.

[3] See Glossary.

[4] See Glossary.

[5] This position, which is called "process theology," is exemplified in the metaphysical works of the English philosopher, Alfred North Whitehead (1861–1947). The most notable contemporary exponent of Whiteheadian process theology is Charles Hartshorne, author of *Philosophers Speak of God* (Chicago, 1953), *The Logic of Perfection* (La Salle, Ill., 1962) and *Aquinas to Whitehead: Seven Centuries of Metaphysics of Religion* (Milawukee, 1976).

[6] This theory is expounded in Freud's *Totem and Taboo*. Freud later expounded the internal psychological mechanisms accounting for the development of the idea of God in *The Future of an Illusion*. According to this account, the idea of God results from the tensions of the Oedipus complex in the young child; as a projection of the superego, it is an attempt to perpetuate the influence of the father in a "transcendental" image; and, insofar as it inhibits the mature functioning of the ego, it is neurosis-inducing.

⁷ Cf. *The Essence of Christianity*, Evans tr. (N.Y., 1957), by Ludwig Feuerbach (1804–1872), Preface.

⁸ Feuerbach's solution to the unhappy alienation caused by the idea of God is to eradicate the God-image from human culture. The anticipated result of this eradication, says Feuerbach, will be the attainment of a genuine sense of love and community among the peoples of the earth, after the wasteful and unhealthy diversion of human love-energy to God had been stemmed. According to Feuerbach, the sciences of psychology and anthropology would play a major part in bringing about these latter beneficial results.

⁹ The quest for the "historical Jesus," which in its 20th century version has been promoted by Albert Schweitzer, Rudolf Bultmann and other theologians and scripture exegetes, is concerned with removing the accretions of myth and legend that have built up around the figure of Jesus Christ over the centuries, and uncovering the unadorned historical personality and message of Jesus.

¹⁰ Religious societies as subordinate to the jurisdiction of political society and the judgements of the "public morality" would be "sub-societies"; but, if they are believed to transcend, or even exert some sort of spitirual or invisible control over, secular society, they might be called "supra-societies."

¹¹ Confucianism, unless it is combined with the independent strain of Taoism, does not emphasize any belief in a transcendent God or Absolute, although it takes ancestor-worshiping for granted. Buddhism, although it is oriented primarily towards the attainment of "Enlightenment" (*Satori*), which bears many similarities to what is called "religious experience," explicitly excludes any adherence to a notion of a transcendent God.

VIII. *"Ethics and Aesthetics"*

¹ See Glossary.

² According to the *Statistical Abstract of the United States* (1974), the male homicide rate in 1957 in the U.S. was 7.6 murders per 100,000 population as compared with 1.4 murders per 100,000 population in Industrialized Western Europe, 0.6 murders in Scandinavia and the Netherlands, 1.5 murders in Canada, and 2.8 murders in Japan. In 1967, the rate per 100,000 population was 11.3 murders in the U.S. as compared with 1.1 murders in Industrialized Western Europe, 0.7 murders in Scandinavia and the Netherlands, 1.9 murders in Canada, and 1.9 murders in Japan. The discrepancy in rates for female homicide between the U.S. and other countries was similarly wide. The United States also greatly surpasses the other countries mentioned in most other forms of violent crime. Cf. also the *Uniform Crime Reports, 1971: Crime in the United States* (Wash., D.C.), and the Council of Europe's report, "Violence in Society," in *Collected Studies in Criminological Research* (Strasboug, 1974).

³ See "Hedonism" in Glossary.

⁴ Cf. e.g. Plato's *Symposium, passim;* and *Phaedrus* (249B-C).

⁵ Kant's aesthetic theory is expounded in his *Critique of Judgment*, Part I.

⁶ Sections 309, 310.

⁷ See "Aesthetics" in Glossary.

⁸ "Transcendental turn" is a Kantian term which in the strict Kantian sense connotes a study of the subjective grounds for the possibility of objective knowledge. However, in a wider sense, the term can be used to describe a turning away from the preoccupation with objective matters to give explicit attention to subjective modes of considering or formulating these objective matters.

⁹ See Glossary.

"*Epilogue*"

[1] Although Herbert Spencer (1820–1903) espoused a utilitarian system of ethics, he claimed that the "happiness" to be attained in his utilitarianism was necessarily associated with behavior contributing to survival.

[2] Moore's basic point was that "good" could not be equated with anything in the natural world, because it is always an "open question" whether that with which it is equated is good or not. For instance, if good is equated with pleasure, one can reasonably ask the question, "but is this or that pleasure good," and so the equation of pleasure with good is still an "open question." Those who made the mistake of making such equations of good with anything natural were said to be guilty of the "Naturalistic fallacy." In order to avoid the naturalistic fallacy, Moore suggested that the good should be considered a "nonnatural" property, i.e. a property not directly experiencable in the world but only accessible to "intuition" (see "Intuitionism" in Glossary).

[3] A naturalistic ethical theory is one which defines the "good" or "right" in terms of some natural entity or experiential fact, e.g. the instinct for survival.

[4] The "is" in this case would be the survival-orientation of ethical statements (as established by metaethical analysis); while the "ought" would be the normative "prescription" that people "ought" to behave in such a way as to promote survival.

[5] See "Pragmatism" in Glossary.

GLOSSARY

(The following Glossary includes some of the more important names and subjects which are referred to in the dialogues between Cranston and Turner, and may not be familiar to the beginning student of ethical theory who reads this book.)

AESTHETICS: A branch of philosophy concerned specifically with the description or formulation of the laws of sensuous appreciation, in particular of works of art, but (depending on the breadth of the aesthetic theory) sometimes also of nature, or persons, etc. (Turner in these dialogues utilizes the term in this latter, broader sense.) Aesthetic theories in art are sometimes classified according to their approach and type of emphasis. For example, *formism* in aethetics emphasizes the imitation of either actual or idealized forms on the part of the artist; *contextualism* focuses primarily on the possibility of enhancement of sensuous qualities through a relationship to their aesthetic environment or context; *organicism* explicitates the commonly-held belief that aesthetic objects should be integrated and harmonious, by advocating an explicit comparison of aesthetic objects with natural organisms (taken as archetypal examples of harmony and self-integration). For a discussion of hedonism as an aesthetic stance, see HEDONISM.

ANTECEDENT and CONSEQUENT: (see DEDUCTION)

ARISTOTLE (398–322 B.C.) defined ethics in terms of the pursuit of happiness, which he identifies with "the good." The main path to the attainment of happiness, aside from personal advantage and good fortune, is the development of habits of intellectual and moral virtues. The intellectual virtues include wisdom, prudence, intuition, scientific reasoning and art. The moral virtues include temperance, courage and justice, all of which consist in one way or another in maintaining a mean between two vicious extremes. For example, temperance is a mean between indifference to pleasure and over-indulgence; and courage is a mean between cowardice and foolhardiness.

AXIOLOGY: The philosophical study of all types of value, ethical, aesthetic, religious, economic, etc. Distinctions are often made between intrinsic values (which are sought for their own sake) and instrumental values (which are sought because they are means to the attainment of some intrinsic value).

BEHAVIORISM, the predominant school of psychology in the U.S., received its first impetus from the study of the salivary reactions of animals by the Russian psychologist, Ivan Pavlov (1849–1936), and was introduced into the intellectual mainstream of the U.S. primarily through the writings of J.B. Watson of John

Hopkins University. Moderate Behavorism tends to suspend judgement about the existence of an "inner" emotional and "mental" life, and to study only publicly observable and measurable actions and reactions in human and animal subjects, for the purpose of understanding and being able to predict human behavior. "Logical" or "dogmatic" behaviorism, a form of materialism, goes even further and denies that there is any "inner" life aside or independent from phenomenally manifested behavioral responses.

CATEGORICAL IMPERATIVE: (see KANT)

"CATEGORY MISTAKE" is a term popularized in contemporary philosophy by Gilbert Ryle, who used the term to refer to the deception and confusion that results when people use two very different types of categories in overtly similar ways, e.g. applying "team spirit" and "good serving and receiving" as if they both promoted a football team's victory in the same way, or (in philosophy) talking about the operations of the mind and bodily actions as if they both belonged to the single category of "activities" in the selfsame way.

CONTEXTUALISM: (see AESTHETICS).

DEDUCTION: The derivation of conclusions from premises in logically admissable ways. For example, if A = B and B = C, we may conclude that A = C. If A is either B or C, and we know that A is not C, then we may conclude that A is B. Conclusions may also be derived from conditional or hypothetical premises: for example, if we know that A is B on condition that C is D, and we also know that A is *not* B, then we can conclude that C is also *not* D. In this example, "C is D" is called the antecedent, since it is the condition; and "A is B" is called the "consequent," since it is the result of the conditioning antecedent. This negative conclusion is the only type of proof that can be derived from a knowledge about the *consequent*. Positive derivations cannot be similarly made on the basis of our knowledge of the consequent. In other words, if we know that C is B, this tells us nothing for sure about whether A *is* B or not.

DEONTOLOGY is derived from the Greek word, *Deon*, which means "duty." A deontological ethics (e.g. the ethics of Kant) characteristically emphasizes the importance of dutiful adherence to the moral law, regardless of favorable or unfavorable consequences. A sort of "act-deontology," which emphasizes immediate dutiful response to a contingent situation, rather than general laws or rules is also conceivable. "Cranston," who gravitates rather consistently to deontology throughout the dialogues in this book, holds a position intermediate between act-deontology and rule-deontology. He insists (especially in the later dialogues) on the importance of personal, subjective dutiful choices, but also (like Kant) wants to locate the grounds for universality and objectivity within the individual subjectivity – and thus contends that the individual, if he probes deeply enough, can come up with individual responses that are not *just* individual, but have a certain universality about them, albeit not the sharply defined universality of explicit rules. Deontological ethics is usually contrasted with "teleological" ethics, which emphasizes the fact that the morality of an action can be judged by the (nonmoral, amoral) consequences which are produced, or are ordinarily produced, or are conjectured as bound to be produced, by that action or that type of action, or the specific application of the moral law that is exemplified through that action.

DESCRIPTIVE ETHICS: is the study of the moral opinions and values actually held by people, or persons, and/or of the types of behavior actually considered moral or immoral by people.

DUTY: (see DEONTOLOGY).

EPISTEMOLOGY: The branch of philosophy concerned with the nature and validity of our knowledge of reality, rather than with the nature of reality itself. An "epistemological" consideration is one which concentrates exclusively on the knowledge or knowability of an object, idea, or objective.

EXISTENTIALISM is a movement with so many variations that it is almost impossible to generalize on. A common theme in Sartre, Camus, and other existentialists is the alienated situation in which the individual finds himself and the need of the individual to freely manifest his "authentic self" in spite of adverse conditions which may surround him or pose obstacles to fulfillment.

FORMALISM: (see AESTHETICS).

HEDONISM: "Psychological" hedonism states that pleasure (or the memory of pleasures, or the idea of pleasure) is the prime motivating factor in human behavior. "Aesthetic" hedonism hypothesizes that the experience of beauty or even aesthetic experiences in a wider sense, consist in an intense and immediate pleasure in something for its own sake. "Ethical" hedonism states that what we call "intrinsic good" or happiness, is synonymous with pleasure; some, but not all ethical hedonists (e.g. some utilitarians) go on to say that actions become "right" or "wrong" depending on whether they are instrumental to the attainment or production of pleasure, or not.

HEGEL: (1770–1831) G.W.F. Hegel was a German philosopher who, after the fashion of the then-prominent "idealist" movement, presented a world-view emphasizing the unity of opposites. In the area of ethics, Hegel emphasized the synthesis of right with duty, good intentions with good consequences, inner ideals with outer expressions, free decisions with natural necessities, and individual morality with social ethics.

HYPOTHETICAL IMPERATIVE: (see KANT).

INDUCTION is the logical process by which we arrive at generalizations after a systematic examination of particular properties of particular objects, or particular processes or events, or particular samples taken to be representative of a whole. Since induction does not require an exhaustive inspection of *all* the particulars under consideration to justify the generalizations made, it is often said that induction yields only probability, not certainty. In other words, it could happen that particulars may turn up contradicting an inductive generalization made in acceptable ways. In this sense, induction contrasts sharply with deduction, which is always certain and noncontradictable, provided that its inferences have been made according to acceptable procedures in logic.

INTUITIONISM: Some ethical intuitionists hold that there are certain ethical generalizations which are valid for all cases, but are so self-evident that they need not, and indeed cannot, be proved through logical reasoning processes. Other intuitionists are simply concerned with emphasizing that our primary source for evaluating the rightness of acts must not be external consequences but internal moral insight.

KANT: (1724–1804) Immanuel Kant is famous in ethics for propounding an "a priori" approach to morality: rightness and wrongness, says Kant, are determined "categorically" by man's practical reason (i.e. will) which formulates valid maxims for behavior and imposes these as norms for all men. The validity of the maxims which are formulated can be tested by each individual if he simply asks himself whether he would will his own maxim for behavior to become the law for all men; if he can will this without self-contradiction, then that maxim has the status of a universal and objectively valid moral law. (This process of testing maxims is one example of the application of what is called the criterion of "universalizability" [q.v.]). The process of testing maxims and selecting only the universalizable ones is also considered to be a kind of triumph of the will over "the inclinations," which tend towards the particular and the selfish, rather than the universal, and thus are a source of conflict. Kant contrasts his "categorical" imperative with the "hypothetical imperative" propounded by many other ethicians. The "hypothetical imperative," rather than imposing laws for human behavior on the basis of their pure rational validity (determined by the appropriate "tests") formulates only conditional laws which depend on whether or not they are conductive to "happiness," which Kant defines as fulfillment of the inclinations. According to a hypothetical imperative, says Kant, an act is moral only if it promotes happiness, and the degree of morality of an act corresponds to the degree of happiness which it produces. Such a mode of determining morality is experimental or "a posteriori," insofar as it depends on either the actual experiences of consequences or the projection of consequences to be experienced in the future; and hypothetical, insofar as it depends on a condition (i.e. whether or not an act produces happiness).

METAETHICS is the study of moral discourse. In particular, it studies the way that we use terms such as "right" and "good," the meanings we attach to such terms, and the standards of reasoning or proof that are applicable to sentences employing such terms. Theoretically, metaethics maintains neutrality in regard to various positions in normative ethics (q.v.), but there is some dispute as to whether complete neutrality can be maintained in practice.

METAPHYSICS in a traditional and very broad sense is a study of whatever is beyond the realm of the observable and merely physical. Thus it is concerned with the existence and nature of God. the mind or soul, the will and freedom, the essences of natures which are considered to be the source of sensible properties, the possibility of human survival after death, and the nature of the world-as-a-whole. Those who deny the reality of non-physical entities or properties, or who deny that the non-physical is knowable, or who deny that meaningful statements can be made about reality as a totality, are generally critical of metaphysics as defined above.

NATURALISM in metaethics (q.v.) is an interpretation of ethical discourse which tends to derive our use of ethical terms such as "ought," "good," and "right" from factual states of affairs. For example, an ethical naturalist might contend that "X is good for me" reducible is to "X gives me pleasure," or that "you ought to do Y" really means "according to the common experience of mankind, Y is to some degree necessary for your survival or the survival of others."

NATURAL LAW is contrasted with positive law. Whereas positive law results from enactments, whether arbitrary or well-considered, made by the relevant authorities in any society, natural law is thought to have an importance and permanence superseding the laws of any particular society and the various needs manifested in that society. This higher supervening law has been defended and justified in various ways: from a regularity in nature itself, which also regulates human actions and interactions; from the mind or will of God, who, as creator of men, has the right to impose on human nature certain common obligations for the attainment of the goals for which men were created; from a sort of common-denominator consensus about what is right and wrong, emerging out of all the various customs and laws prevailing among the nations; from some initial "natural state" of primitive man, or man considered in abstraction from, or prior to, the complex modern societies he has formed; or from the exigencies of reason or logic itself, which dictates that only certain general principles can be maintained consistently and without self-contradiction. An important function of natural law in history is that it has provided a "court of appeal" for men who believed that certain actually prevailing positive laws were tyrannical or unjust.

NONCOGNITIVISM in contemporary metaethics takes issue with any attempt to justify ethical assertions in terms of *knowledge*, whether knowledge of facts, or knowledge of the logical consistency and non-self-contradiction of ethical reasons, or immediate intuitive suprasensory or extrasensory knowledge. Ethical statements are generally interpreted very subjectively by noncognitivists – as expressions of emotions, or of approval; or as mere commands or exhortations; or as the arbitrary recommendation or even imposition of certain values.

NORMATIVE ETHICS is concerned with making generalizations about the way people actually *should* act, or the motives that *should* influence them, or the attitudes that *should* pervade their behavior. Insofar as the "should" (or "ought") of normative statements implies some imposition or obligatoriness, howsoever strong or weak, these statements may be called "prescriptive" statements, to differentiate them from the descriptive statements in ethics (see DESCRIPTIVE ETHICS) which are concerned only with conveying the bare factual situation.

ONTOLOGY ("a study of being") is sometimes contrasted with logic ("a study of reasoning processes") or with epistemology ("a study of knowledge or truth"). An "ontological consideration" in the context of such a contrast becomes a consideration or treatment which emphasizes the existence or reality of something, rather than its logical justifiability, knowability or verifiability.

PLATO (438–348 B.C.) emphasized the importance of a knowledge of the Good, for ethical activity. The Good, as he defined it, was a transcendent Idea which gave rise to all sensuous reality and even to all other ideas, and is similar in conception to the idea of God in some philosophies and religions. The Idea of the Good could only be known intuitively and participated in by the sage or philosopher who had undergone a long preliminary process of "dialectical" education, in which he uses art, music, science, mathematics and philosophical and ethical inquiry to rise above immersion in sensuous things to the vision of the Good and the interrelation and coordination of all other major Ideas subordinated to the Good. Since the knowledge of the Good and Ideas related to the Good caused a necessary *attraction* to the Good and pursuit of the Good, the philosopher-dialectician's knowledge of the Good would not be simply abstract and theoretical, but would necessarily impel him to engage in good activities, i.e. the cultivation of the moral virtues, temperance, courage, prudence and justice, and to impart his insights to others.

POSITIVE LAW: (see NATURAL LAW).

PRAGMATISM in ethics was propounded primarily by William James (1842–1910) and John Dewey (1859–1952). In James' version the emphasis was on the fact that the "truth" of our values and moral beliefs depends in the last analysis on the relative satisfaction and fulfillment they are calculated to bring to us. Dewey refined such suggestive ideas into an "instrumentalist" theory of ethics, according to which ethical judgements are responses to problems, tensions or conflicts which an individual experiences in relationship to his environment, and the "warranted assertions" or truths of ethics are the "pragmatic" solutions he arrives at – solutions which are characterized by flexibility, adaptibility, conduciveness towards personal growth, and lack of prepossession by any fixed or outmoded ideas, ends, or principles. Pragmatism, like most forms of utilitarianism, is a "naturalistic" ethical theory (q.v.) insofar as it defines the good or the moral in terms of a certain species of factual experience to be attained; however, at least in its Deweyan formulation, it differs from utilitarianism in its built-in resistance to any kind of concern with goals or ends (the only end, according to Dewey, is growth itself, and what we call "ends" are just means to further refining our moral hypotheses); in its quasi-scientific emphasis on the "pragmatic criterion," which (in very general terms) involved the verification of ethical "hypotheses" in and through practical experience (this emphasis becomes particularly explicit in the discussion of values in Deweyan educational theories); and in its emphasis on biological-psychological conflicts and tension leading to puzzlement, conation and eventual surmountal of a problem (an emphasis reflecting Dewey's own prepragmatic interest in both biology and Hegelian dialectics).

PRAGMATIC CRITERION: (see PRAGMATISM)
PRESCRIPTIVISM: (see NORMATIVE ETHICS)
TELEOLOGICAL ETHICS: (see DEONTOLOGY)
UNIVERSALIZABILITY, CRITERION OF: The "universalizability criterion" is the testing of normative moral assertions for universality. For example, one might want to test the statement "X is morally permissable" by asking, "is X *always* permissable?" In some formulations of universalizations, the questioner might also want to add, "is X permissable for *all* men? at *all times?* in all circumstances?" etc. The supposition here is that, if one can answer an unqualified "yes" to such questions even for a few moral norms, such moral norms would have a special claim to objectivity and validity because of their very universality. In the Kantian Categorical Imperative (q.v.), which is frequently given as an example of the universalizability criterion, there is special emphasis on non-self-contradiction as the key to true universality; i.e., the Kantian is particularly interested in asking, "is it possible, without *self-contradiction*, to will that all men do X?" The universalizability criterion is usually applied in connection with deontological ethical systems but may also be applied in the case of teleological systems (q.v.): for example, a utilitarian (q.v.) might pose the question, "would you *like* to see X established as a universal law for everyone?" Since the use of the verb, "like" here is an implicit appeal to the goal of satisfaction or happiness, which is a central concept in utilitarianism, this would be a distinctively utilitarian formulation of the universalizability criterion.

UTILITARIANISM: is an ethical theory which gauges the rightness or wrongness of action on the basis of whether these actions produce good or bad consequences, and thus is a "teleological theory of ethics. "Act" utilitarianism is concerned with the consequences of individual acts, while "rule" utilitarianism is concerned with the consequences of certain species of action, i.e. certain rules for acting. "Egotistic" utilitarianism is concerned with consequences to the individual, while "universalistic" utilitarianism is interested in consequences affecting a community, society, or the world as a whole. "Hedonistic" utilitarianism equates "good consequences" with pleasure, and "bad consequences" with pain, while "idealistic" utilitarianism allows that some good consequences may not be pleasurable, and some pleasurable consequences may not be good – in other words, it tends to hold to higher standards for good than "mere" pleasure. Utilitarianism may be either descriptive or normative. Descriptive utilitarianism says that people in the world actually *do* judge moral goodness or badness on the basis of consequences. Normative utilitarianism states that people *ought* to judge moral goodness and badness in this way (which may imply that they often do *not* make their judgements in this way). The English philosopher, Jeremy Bentham (1748–1832) is usually considered the founder of modern utilitarian ethics, although Bishop Richard Cumberland (1631–1718), Francis Hutchenson (1694–1747) and David Hume (1711–1776) were important forerunners of utilitarianism in the British Isles. Bentham was a normative universalistic hedonistic act-utilitarian. John Stuart Mill (1806–1873), his intellectual successor, is harder to classify in terms of the above-mentioned distinctions. He tended towards universalism, but (even more than Bentham) attempted to show that universalistic altruism and benevolence was compatible with, and even derivable from, egotistic psychological hedonism; he tended towards idealism, but wanted to portray idealistic goods as rather "high-level" pleasures; he is often interpreted as being a rule-utilitarian (the "act" and "rule" distinction came into vogue only after Mill's death), but some of the evidence used to back up this interpretation could also be used to show he was an act-utilitarian. He definitely proposed utilitarianism as a normative theory, but also seemed to presuppose that utilitarian moral judgements are the most "natural" to men, i.e. the kind of processes that normal people go through in making judgements of morals. "Turner" in the dialogues in this book tends toward utilitarianism from both a metaethical and a normative vantage point. That is, he believes that ethical discourse is best interpreted in utilitarian fashion; and also recommends utilitarian principles as a guide to human activity. Like Mill, he is hard to describe in terms of the usual categories: He tends towards a position which has sometimes been called "actual-rule-utilitarianism," which emphasizes actually prevailing rules in society. But Turner would include unwritten customs and matters of social consensus under the heading of "rules"; would extend the definition of "society" to include dissenting sub-groupings, special interest groups and supranational organizations; and would insist that conformity to actual rules does not determine "*intrinsic*" morality (something that Turner takes to be imaginary, or at least unknowable, or at the very least undiscussable).

BIBLIOGRAPHY

Argyle, Michael, *Religious Behavior* (Glencoe, Ill., 1958).

Aristotle, *Nichomachean Ethics* and *Topics* from *The Basic Works of Aristotle*, McKeon ed. (N.Y., 1941).

Baum, Archie, "Aesthetic Experience and Moral Experience," *Journal of Philosophy*, LV, 20, Sept., 1958.

Bourke, Vernon, J., *The History of Ethics*, Vols. I & II (Garden City, N.Y., 1968).

Cassirer, Ernst, *Determinism and Interdeminism in Modern Physics*, O. Benfey tr. (N.Y., 1956).

Devlin, Sir Patrick, *The Enforcement of Morals* (London, 1959).

Dewey, John, *Human Nature and Conduct* (N.Y., 1922).
—, *The Quest for Certainty* (N.Y., 1922).

Evans, J.D.G., *Aristotle's Concept of Dialectic* (Cambridge, 1977).

Flew, A.G.N., *Evolutionary Ethics* (London, 1967).

Frankena, W.K. *Ethics* (Englewood Cliffs, N.J., 1963).

Freud, Sigmund, *The Ego and the Id*, Strachey ed. (N.Y., 1960).

Gewirth, Alan, *Moral Rationality* (N.Y., 1972).

Gilson, Etienne, "The Idea of God and the Difficulties of Atheism," in *The Great Ideas Today*, Hutchins and Adler eds. (Chicago, 1969).

Hannaford, R.V., "You 'Ought' to Derive Ought from 'Is' " in *Ethics* LXXXII, 2, Jan. 1972).

Hart, H.M., Jr., "*The Aims of Criminal Law*," in *Law and Contemporary Problems* (Durham, N.C., 1958).

Hart, H.L.A., "Social Solidarity and the Enforcement of Morality," in *Ethics and Public Policy*, T. Beauchamp ed. (Englewood Cliffs, N.J., 1975).

Harris, Errol E., "Dialectic and Scientific Method," in *Idealistic Studies* III, 1, Jan. 1973.

Hegel, G.W.F., *The Philosophy of Right*, T.M. Knox tr. (Oxford, 1942).

Hobbes, Thomas, *Leviathan*, Molesworth ed. (London, 1839).

Hudson, W.D. ed., *The Is-Ought Question* (N.Y., 1969).

Hume, David, *Enquiry Concerning the Principles of Morals*, C.W. Hendel ed. (N.Y., 1957).
—, *A Treatise of Human Nature*, III, Selby-Bigge ed. (Oxford 1896).

James, William, *Pragmatism* and four essays from *The Meaning of Truth*, compiled by R.B. Perry (Cleveland, 1968).

Kainz, Howard P., "The Aesthetic Theory in Hegel's *Phenomenology of Spirit*, in *Idealistic Studies* I, 2, April, 1971.
—, "Kierkegaard's 'Three Stages' and the Levels of Spiritual Maturity," in *The Modern Schoolman* LII, 4, June 1975.

Kamenka, *Marxism and Ethics* (N.Y., 1969).

Kant, Immanuel, *Fundamental Principles of the Metaphysic of Morals*, Abbot tr. (N.Y., 1949).

Kierkegaard, Søren, *Either/Or*, Swensen tr. (Garden City, N.Y., 1959).

Lacroix, Jean, *The Meaning of Modern Atheism*, Garret Barden tr. (Dublin, 1965).

Leiser, B.M., *Liberty, Justice and Morals* (N.Y., 1973).

Mac Intyre, A. and Ricoeur, P., *The Religious Significance of Atheism* (N.Y., 1969).

Mill, J.S., *Utilitarianism* (London, 1861).
—, *The Utility of Religion* (London, 1923).

Moore, G.E., *Ethics* (London, 1912).
—, *Principia Ethica* (Cambridge, 1903).

Myrdal, Gunnar, *An American Dilemma* (N.Y., 1974).

Nietzsche, Friedrick, *Thus Spake Zarathustra*, in *The Philosophy of Nietzsche* (N.Y., 1927).

O'Connor, D.J., *Aquinas and Natural Law* (London, 1967).

Olafson, F., *Ethics and Twentieth Century Thought* (Englewood Cliffs, N.J., 1973).

Parsons, Talcott, *The Structure of Social Action* (Glencoe, Illinois, 1949).

Perry, R.B., *General Theory of Value* (Boston, 1926).

Plato, *Republic*, in *The Dialogues of Plato*, Jowett tr. (N.Y., 1892).

Pound, Roscoe, *Law and Morals* (Chapel Hill, N.C., 1924).

Prichard, H.A., "Does Moral Philosophy Rest on a Mistake?" in *Mind* XXI, 1912.

Read, Herbert, *Education through Art* (London, 1943).

Ross, W.D., *The Foundations of Ethics* (Oxford, 1939).
—, *The Right and the Good* (Oxford, 1930).

Sheldon, Wm., *The Varieties of Temperament* (N.Y., 1942).

Sidgwick, Henry, *The Methods of Ethics*, C. Jones ed. (Chicago, 1962).

Singer, Marcus, *Generalization in Ethics* (N.Y., 1961).

Skinner, B.F., *Science and Human Behavior*, (N.Y., 1953).

Sumner, W.G., *Folkways* (Boston, 1907).

Warnock, Mary, *Existentialist Ethics* (London, 1967).

Warnock, G.J., *Contemporary Moral Philosophy* (London, 1967).

Wittgenstein, "A Lecture in Ethics," in *The Philosophical Review* LXXIV, 1, Jan. 1, 1965).

SUBJECT INDEX

Abbreviations
DM ought = moral obligation from duty
    f = following pages (1 or 2)
    ff = following pages (2 or more)
    fn = first note
HM ought = moral obligation from happiness
    m = moral
    n = note
    sn = second note
    T = temperamental

NAME INDEX